FROM NORTH YORKSHIRE

Edited by Emma Marsden

First published in Great Britain in 2000 by
YOUNG WRITERS
Remus House,
Coltsfoot Drive,
Woodston,
Peterborough, PE2 9JX
Telephone (01733) 890066

HB ISBN 0 75431 952 0
SB ISBN 0 75431 953 9

FOREWORD

This year, the Young Writers' Future Voices competition proudly presents a showcase of the best poetic talent from over 42,000 up-and-coming writers nationwide.

Successful in continuing our aim of promoting writing and creativity in children, our regional anthologies give a vivid insight into the thoughts, emotions and experiences of today's younger generation, displaying their inventive writing in its originality.

The thought, effort, imagination and hard work put into each poem impressed us all and again the task of editing proved challenging due to the quality of entries received, but was nevertheless enjoyable. We hope you are as pleased as we are with the final selection and that you continue to enjoy *Future Voices From North Yorkshire* for many years to come.

CONTENTS

The Poems

My Little Brother!

Playing with the Action Men,
Inside the camouflaged, dusty den,
Sat a boy of ten,
Oh how he loved his Action Men.

He is my little pesty brother,
How he does look like my mother.
I could honestly say he's her twin,
But he's so scruffy, like a used bin.

He sometimes invites me to his room,
To play hide and seek in dark and gloom.
So I do sometimes say 'Yes, yes, yes,'
But I wish he wouldn't be a pest.

Mother makes us light chocolate cakes,
Then he wants to mix and bake.
Chocolate's all around his face,
Especially on his bow-tie lace.

My little brother is now 12 years old,
His ambition is to go to the South Pole.
I realise now he is quite nice,
But dear brother, get rid of those *mice!*

Victoria Branley (12)

Food Haiku

I like fish and chips
They are really tasty with
Salt and vinegar!

I hate broccoli
It is really disgusting
It makes me feel sick!

I like hamburgers
Especially with mustard
(But I hate gherkins!)

I *love* eating sweets
They make my teeth all sticky
I can't talk any more!

Rosalind Skinner (13)

Pink

Pink is sugar-coated fancies,
Cosy love on hazy days,
Downy pillows just fluffed up,
A china rose, a loving gaze.

Pink is sweetness on your tongue,
Melting ice-cream in your hand,
The ballet dancer's fluffed up tutu,
Fairies from another land.

Pink is like playful cuddles,
Sweet, soft-centred strawberry creams,
Feathery boa round your neck,
Ice-pink lipstick, lazy dreams.

Please help me, I cannot think,
What the world would be without pink.

Natalie Atkinson (13)
Barlby High School

SCHOOL

S chool is the greatest
C ool, I love school
H ey, I missed school, *aaaggghhh*
O h yippee, school is there
O h no, I missed school, what am I going to do?
L earning is great, I don't know how people
can hate it so much.

I love Boroughbridge High School
S ummer term is here, no more school.
I'm bored out of my head. How could anyone
live without school because I know I can't,
I'm bored.

G reat, school is back
R E is my favourite lesson
E nglish is alright
A hhh, I'm very sick
T he weekend is here. I need to do my homework
I love it.

Craig Ritchie (13)
Boroughbridge High School

The Snake

S idewinder
N asty
A dder
K inky
E ver hunting

C areful
A nd
S linky
C arcasses
A nd
B lood
L izards beware
E ver eating.

Tim Morrill (12)
Boroughbridge High School

Snake Acrostic

S lithering, curvy, long and windy is the snake
N eedle-fanged, it shows its teeth off proudly
A snake is patterned to camouflage and hide from you
K iller, the snake
E asing through the desert it goes looking for its prey
S ee its beady eyes and liquorice tongue waiting, waiting
in the long grass.

Samantha Thompson (12)
Boroughbridge High School

School Is Boring

S chool is sad, the locker area is mad
C ookos can't cook
H orrible teachers
O h, not to mention the dinners are covered in hairs
O ur school is cramped
L ockers get kicked in

I really hate school
S chool dinners are sad

B ob is the man to get the answer
O ld dinner bags are so fat
R E teachers are funny creatures when they are mad
I f you don't work, you will be so thick
N o one wants to go
G eography teachers are so fat and sad.

Shaun Stevenson (13)
Boroughbridge High School

Snake

The slithering snake approached me
I jumped back with surprise
The limbless treacherous reptile
With his vampire fangs, flickering tongue
And his wide beady eyes.

I just stood there startled,
Not even daring to move
I stared at the scaly creature,
How dangerous that could prove.

Melanie Blackburn (12)
Boroughbridge High School

THE SNAKE

While standing by the lake
I was startled by a snake
Coming out from under a bush

Its scaly body eased its way towards me
It slowly coiled its way up a tree
Then *snap*, he had his lunch

As I tried to move slowly away
His beady eyes caught sight of me as he lay
And I froze with sheer fright

His vampire teeth shone in the light
Then the next thing I knew
Snap!

Kirsty Bryant (12)
Boroughbridge High School

THE SNAKE

The snake, sinister, prowling through the grass,
masterfully hunting its prey.
Eyes glaring, its complex, dynamic design
keeps it hidden.
It sways, it snarls, dazzling with fatality.

The sinister snake, spots its unfortunate one.
Venomous, fatal strike is all it takes.
It spikes its prey with poisoned fangs,
leaving trails of blood behind.

Wendy Crehore (12)
Boroughbridge High School

A Hunter Who Is Hunted

They're hunted,
Pursued,
Tracked down,
Killed.
Haunted by the human race.
But they're survivors,
Always have been.
Their bite is dangerous,
Or harmless.
They bite when bitten,
Leaving their victim crisp,
As when living.
Through the centuries
Either hated,
Or worshipped.
Sliding down ages,
Creeping through civilisations,
But alive.
Hearts that beat,
Lungs that heave,
And living!

Madeleine Orange (12)
Boroughbridge High School

Snake

S is for slithering along the floor
N is for nowhere to be seen
A is for attack that happens so fast
K is for killing to catch the rat
E is for eating down in one gulp.

Jonathan Hardie (12)
Boroughbridge High School

We Are All The Same

If you dig a hole
and I dig a hole
you will be paid more than I

and if you lift some coal
and I lift some coal
the pay is different, why?

If men and women can do the same job
and they are the same as each other,
then why is the pay so much different
which they try so hard to cover.

I try to tell them that the wages are different
but they just turn and walk away,
I won't be able to find a good job
but I can't stand this anymore.
No way!

Helen Marshall (14)
Boroughbridge High School

The Way They Move

The way it glides and lurches,
Weaving its way down, down,
Slithering, sucking up a priority,
Moving and shedding its skin.

Roaming the hillsides,
Rattling its movements,
Licking its skin,
And watching for predators.

Rachael Burley (12)
Boroughbridge High School

THE SNAKE

Never ever misjudge a snake
You can never tell if they are venomous or not
They could eat you alive,
Or they could just strangle you instead,
Or even they might just give you
A horrible sharp bite.
So just be careful,
Never ever misjudge a snake.

Sometimes they can be nice,
They just slither their way around you.
They are quite stunning until
They turn around and bite you.
So just be careful,
Never ever misjudge a snake.

Rachel Johnson (12)
Boroughbridge High School

THE SNAKE

B old and wide,
O ld and withered,
O h, only poisonous if they bite,
M ade of dry scales,
S ome deadly, some harmless,
L ong or short,
A ngry or shy
N o, don't be afraid,
G reen mamba snakes only come out
at night!

Emma Cundall (12)
Boroughbridge High School

Hamadryads & Mambas

H amadryads are scary
A re you afraid?
M ambas are green and daunting
A re you afraid?
D aunting eyes motionless
R eady to kill its defenceless prey
Y ou are its prey
A re you afraid?
D on't look back, it's coming to get you.

Motionless is the snake
Hungry it is
Eyeing up a tasty snack
Waiting for its prey to crack
The prey moves
The snake moves too
The prey is gone
The snake waits
For something else to come.

S nakes are lovely
N ice and quiet
A nd seeing as you are daring
K iss its face
E nd of your life, here it comes
S nakes can kill, didn't I tell you?

Hannah Taylor (12)
Boroughbridge High School

A Poem About School

S chool is boring
C rowds are forming in the playground
H orrible teachers setting me homework
O n the way to school
O n a bus that always breaks down
L earning to write

I 'm so bored
S chool is so boring

S ATs are a pain
A nd I'll be revising again
D reading the next day at school.

Michael Abbott (13)
Boroughbridge High School

Snakes

S limy reptiles looking for prey
N asty looking things hunting
A cid-throwing reptiles
K illers in the wild
E nding little mammals' lives
S crounging for more prey.

James Belchamber (12)
Boroughbridge High School

Snakes

Snakes are slithery,
They are ill-natured and bad tempered.
Their ferocious bites can sometimes be fatal.

As they slowly glide up towards their prey,
They plan carefully what they should do.
A fast approach gives the prey no chance to get away.

I hate their gigantic fangs inside their grand mouth,
Their flat and unwrinkled skin allows them to squirm in and out
of small places.

You never know where they will be next!

Emily Rowe (13)
Boroughbridge High School

Snakes

Snakes, the world's horrible enemy,
things you couldn't imagine or see.
The hissing and sharp eyes,
Ah, the eyes you never know, it spies.
It slithers and at night it creeps,
It creeps when everyone sleeps.
And most of all its bite,
It runs away from people, out of sight.
The rattlesnake, it rattles for a warning,
For its bite is scary, really it's gnawing.
So I'll say goodbye,
Hope snakes aren't spies.

Christopher Nicholls (12)
Boroughbridge High School

The Snake

The snake lives in a warm place
It moves around by a way of skimming
Its flickering tongue and eyes glimmering
With names like boomslang,
Coach whip and indigo.
The rattle of some snakes
Means get up and go.
Some snakes have a colourful pose
But the venom spits out like water in a hose.
Snake!

Michael Horner (12)
Boroughbridge High School

The Snakes Move

The slimy snake slithers sneakily.
Sharp, alert and active.
Sensing all types of fear,
Hearing all types of sounds,
Making its way across the forest,
Zigzagging across the ground.
Over twigs, towards the sound,
The heat of people makes it curve and twist.
This snake will not stop at anything,
Looking for warmth for the night.
Bite, bite, bite.

Jessica Penn (12)
Boroughbridge High School

SLITHERING SLIPPERY SNAKES

A naconda
N astily stalking
A way it glides across the sand
C ool and cold
O h, how it zigs and zags
N eedle-like fangs
D angerous they are
A naconda

H amadryad
A lways there
M ean
A nd
D angerous
R eady to strike
Y awning
A lways there
D anger in the grass.

S limy and slithery
I nteresting walk
D arting this way and that
E asing its way through the grass
W inding about
I nteresting bite
N asty bite
D eadly and venomous
E asing along with a
R eally long tongue.

A lways ready
D arting at you
D eadly bite
E ver
R eady.

S lithering
N eedle fangs
A naconda, adder
K illing
E very day
S limy.

Liam Croft (12)
Boroughbridge High School

WHY DO WE NEED TO GO TO SCHOOL?

Why must we go to school Mummy?
Tell us dear Mummy, please do,
I need to know.
Mummy knows best.

Why must we go to school Daddy?
Tell us dear Daddy, please do,
I need to know.
Daddy knows best.

To learn lots and lots
And get a good reputation
So that you can get a better job
When you're older.

To find all the teachers something to do,
So I've heard the rumour
That goes around the school.
My darling, now buzz off to bed.

Nicola Beadle & Fiona Skilbeck (13)
Boroughbridge High School

SNAKE

S nake hissing, with its
N eedle fangs
A nd its beady eyes looking at me
K illing innocent puppies, rabbits etc
E ven though they kill, they have to live!

Lindsay Winder (12)
Boroughbridge High School

A Pass Through School

In year seven I came to school
The other years thought they were cool
Sometimes I was scared
It's not as if no one cared.

In year eight I came to school
But this time I wasn't a fool
I didn't let everyone push me around
I didn't walk round with a frown.

In year nine I came to school
We were told not to forget our tools
The work was hard
But we still came up the yard.

In year ten I came again
And of course I didn't forget my pen
One more year to do
But I will enjoy it though.

Gina Metcalf (14)
Boroughbridge High School

Snakes!

S nakes can be poisonous but some can be harmless,
N ever go near them because of their bite, they might even kill you!
A nacondas and pythons are threatening only if you tease them,
K ittens and puppies are targets for snakes, so I'd keep away
if I were you,
E ither you love them or you don't, it's all up to you!

Patrick Jordan (12)
Boroughbridge High School

School's Out

The school bell goes,
The children rise,
'That's it everybody' the teacher says
As the children wave goodbye.

Bags are grabbed,
Pulling, pushing, everyone
Trying to get out.

The bus doors open,
Children jump on,
Fights for the front seat,
Now everyone's on.

The school seems empty,
Left alone,
Only the hamster
Sat on its own.

Daniel Jones (13)
Boroughbridge High School

Slither

S lithering unnoticed quietly in the grass
L ike it's hungry for something
I t sees its prey - a sparrow
T he poor thing didn't see it coming
H ungry no more, it returns to its lair
E ntering, it starts to coil itself
R eeling and writhing until it finally falls asleep.

Joseph Ellam (12)
Boroughbridge High School

Top Totty

You walk around like you own the place,
With girls' jaws dropping to the floor.
Your attention's caught by a pretty face,
But you don't care for anything more.

You told Melinda she's the only one,
And Jane you're hers once and for all.
Whilst the whole time you're seeing Emma secretly,
Behind the bike shed wall.

And no sooner have they fallen for you,
With those sparkling eyes and gorgeous hair,
You've lost interest, you've pulled, she's yesterday's news,
You've broken her heart,
But do you care?

Well we've had enough of your little games,
We've caught on to what you do.
We've seen past your eyes and that smarmy disguise,
Now there's no one that loves you but you.

Jade Hutchinson (15)
Boroughbridge High School

Snake Eyes

S lippery, slimy, ugly things
N asty fierce eyes to see with
A cross the floor it slowly winds
K iller by name, killer by nature
E nemy to all small rodents.

Jonathan Glaser (12)
Boroughbridge High School

People At My School

There was an old teacher
Her name was Mrs Preacher
Her mother was a creature
If she was mad, she might even eat yer

There was a new boy
He looked like a toy
You would pull his string
And he's say 'Oh'

There was a big freak
His name was Martin Greek
He was a bit of a geek
But he missed school for a week.

Ben Greenwood (13)
Boroughbridge High School

The Asp

Here she comes,
Winding from side to side,
She must be in a hurry,
For she's doing that slithery slide!
She slides through the sands,
And then into the grass,
And that was the last I heard
Of that sneaky little asp!

Marie Morrison (12)
Boroughbridge High School

Pots And Pans

I have had enough,
Slave labour?
Cleaning and cooking.

Your mess I have tidied
Your bed I have made
Your pots and pans I have scrubbed.

So long I have taken
To do all your chores
But of course, no applause.

You can take your pots and pans
And go scrub them.
I've had enough.

Lyndsey Gibson (14)
Boroughbridge High School

Snakes

S lippery snakes are nasty
N asty snakes are slippery
A cid-injecting smelly snakes
K illing snakes are horrid
E nding lives
S melly, disgusting reptiles.

Will Deadman (12)
Boroughbridge High School

I'VE HAD ENOUGH

I've had enough,
All they say is stuff,
They say it's learning,
But it's just them earning.

I've had enough,
I'm always in a huff.
They get mad,
And I get bad.

I've had enough, of mates,
They all have bad traits.
They are on their chairs
Gathered in pairs.

I've had enough,
I don't care!

Anita Fisher (14)
Boroughbridge High School

A DIFFERENT CREATURE

What an interesting kind of creature,
With lots of dazzling and patterned features.
They can do lots of things like coil up into balls,
Some very big, some very small.
It comes to you with a striking glide,
You don't have to worry, you don't have to hide.
It slides across the floor with an elastic slither,
Even sometimes this can make you shiver.
This makes some interested, some shake,
But altogether this is real, it is the snake.

Meryl Flynn (12)
Boroughbridge High School

CM IN YEAR 8

Disaster strikes!
CM are in year 8.
A year's whizzed by and the form's gone wild.
Emma's now a redhead,
Beep! We can't repeat what Jamie's just said.
Natty's skirt is getting smaller,
Claire's getting even taller.

That's not the end, there's more of us,
Christine's had it with Siobhan,
Conswaila, oops I mean Conway,
Sarah's having a well good day,
James Ellis, whoops he's gone,
Simon's been sent out of the form.

That's not the end, there's more of us,
Stephen Hall drives us up the wall,
George still prays that he was tall,
Mandy is still very handy,
Lizzy's still eating that candy,
Amy's tuft is growing longer.

That's not the end, there's more of us,
Johnson's still annoying us,
Julian always misses the bus,
Sibby's in love with Harry Potter,
Sarah thinks she's getting hotter,
Alix has got very neat writing.

That's not the end, there's more of us,
Petchy's mad about Megan,
Sam's getting soppier,
Harriet's being a copier,
Naomi is a horse fanatic,
Jonathan reads all the books in the attic.

That's not the end, there's more of us,
Smithy's decided he fancies Claire,
John Thompson's lost his underwear,
Gazza's back from holiday,
Twig's having a minta day,
Oh, and there's Adam, the blondy.

That's not the end, there's one more,
the leader of the gang,
It's Mrs M!

Alix McKenna, Amy Howdle, Lizzy Haynes,Sarah Dean,
Harriet Rogerson (12) & Naomi Sherwood (13)
Brayton High School

In The Sky

In the sky,
So very high,
Is so big and blue,
Like some big blue eyes.

In the sky,
The clouds go by,
Big and fluffy,
In my eyes.

It has become night,
Which is not light,
But the stars in the sky,
Are so, so bright,
In my eyes.

David Westwood (12)
Brayton High School

SCIENCE IS MY FAVOURITE SUBJECT

Science is my favourite subject,
There's a lot of fun things to do.
Messing about does have an effect,
So you have to do what you're told to do.

Science is split into different topics,
From chemicals to the moon.
We have used materials such as metal and synthetic,
And are learning more about them soon.

We have done about the reproductive system,
For humans and the plants.
We have learnt about the stamen,
And the stigma which makes other plants.

We have done some experiments,
Using chemicals and heat.
We dropped the Bunsen and made a dent,
It only just missed my feet.

We have leant about the periodic table,
And all the different elements.
It has a lot of different labels,
Showing which is which element.

Science really is my favourite subject.

Stephanie Shipley (12)
Brayton High School

THE HASTINGS DISASTER!

In 1066 Edward the Confessor died.
He had no son to take his name and be king, and so,
Harold Haraada, Harold Godwinson and William Duke
of Normandy each thought that *they* should be.

I didn't take any notice of all this rubbish, until
someone asked me, 'Well, who do you think it should be?'
I thought for a while and said, 'Well, powerful Harold G.
He could make England whatever he wanted it to be,
he'll do for me.'

A battle began somewhere in the North,
With a crash and a bang and a, 'Watch out for your head!'
Harold Haraada soon was dead.

Two left, and
At last for William the Well Prepared, the wind did change.
He landed in the South 300 miles away.
Harold G thought *he* was the best, *he* didn't need a rest.
'Oh no,' cried his troops, 'not another march, not another battle!'

William's plans paid off; well trained troops, a few tricks
and the crown was his.
Oh what a disaster, Harold G, the brave fool, should have won.
For how different would things have been
if we'd had *him* for a king?

Claire Warren (11)
Brayton High School

But Miss!

Sit down.
Shut up.
Pens out.

Right! Today we're gonna . . .
But Miss . . .
Please don't shout.

Sit up.
Close your mouths.
Turn around.

Right! Today we're gonna . . .
But Miss . . .
Please don't make a sound.

Sit straight.
Shut up.
Face this way.

Right! Today we're gonna . . .
But Miss . . .
Please can I have my say.

Stop talking.
Open your books.
Look at me.

Right! Today we're gonna . . .
But Miss . . .
What!
It's twenty past three.

Sarah Atkinson (15)
Brayton High School

THE RIVER

Flowing with grace on rushing tides
Swirling and frothing as it races by
Bubbling and splashing with fishes that ride
The never-ending stream that hisses as it glides.

Like me the river has moods
Sometimes it can knock things over like an almighty hand
Then it sighs as it brushes slowly and softly past the river banks
Or it can be shy and dry up, not to be seen for a long time.

Marching like a platoon of soldiers
Marching to meet the sea
Marching to meet the sea to wage war on piers, cliffs,
and beaches of the world.
It either plods along slowly and orderly or rushes,
losing men as it goes.

But then as man comes into play, the grace, the bubbling and rushing
all cease.
A great dam is lowered, banishing the river to lie forever
Never to wage war or to knock things aside
But to wait peacefully and calmly
for all eternity.

Jonathan Thomas (13)
Fyling Hall School

The Tiger

Fiery red, yet black as night,
The tiger prowls in all his might.
His giant paws,
His sharpened claws,
Proud and brave, a frightening sight.

On the vast, dry plain he wanders around,
Muscles bulging, making no sound.
He likes to run,
In the blazing sun,
Over the rusty, dusty ground.

Lurking and creeping, he sneaks behind,
The antelope herds he desires to find,
He leaps on his prey,
Rips life away,
He gnaws and devours as the bones grind.

Kerry Miller (13)
Fyling Hall School

The Zoo

As it gets closer to feeding time
The animal song begins to rhyme.
The elephants, monkeys and chimpanzees
All call out 'Dinner please.'

The tall giraffe pops out his head
While the lions and tigers roar from their bed.
Bears and pandas shake the trees
And add their voices 'Dinner please.'

The hungry bird flies from his nest
The mighty gorilla pounds on his chest.
The zebras and rhinos fall to their knees
Begging and pleading 'Dinner please.'

The zoo-keeper trudges with buckets of food
Starting his round in a cheerful mood.
When all is done the keeper goes home
And the animals munch and crunch on a bone.

Natasha Hartley (14)
Fyling Hall School

THE SEA

Splashing, swirling and smashing
Flowing, glowing and blowing
Sweeping, tearing and mashing
Waves of the sea come crashing

Grumbling, rumbling and tumbling
Shattering, cracking and creaking
Angry, raging and roaring
Violent the sea comes thundering

Soft, still and amicable
Calm, quiet and peaceable
Tranquil, gentle and likeable
But the waves of the sea are not explicable.

Laura Hamnett (14)
Fyling Hall School

Seven Ages Of Woman

Babies are sweet
With cute, pink feet
But they are annoying
When they start screaming and bawling
Babies are defenceless
Yet often quite monstrous
Children are knowledgeable
About things that are probable
Intrigued about school
But homework – that's just cruel
Scrappy and flappy
Until bullies make them unhappy
Teenagers are ambivalent
About growing up, looking magnificent
They don't like responsibilities
Yet worry about liabilities
Being young and in love
Like a shining white dove
Getting married is nice
Like sugar and spice
But it can soon turn sour
Like a sad, faded flower
Then middle-age sets in
With a great big grin
You're healthy and thriving
At least not dying
Your home grows colder
Your children are older
And are leaving the nest
You think that's best

Now elderly and losing health
Mental and physical abilities are failing
Slowing down quickly
Your body is ailing
Wrinkly and crinkly
Crouched in a chair
With only memories for company
Sparse, wispy hair
Could be dying at last
Mind losing its sense
Like a tree sheds its leaves
Parkinson's disease
From my head down to my knees
Visitors talk over you
Not meaning to be cruel
The seven ages of woman
Please don't ignore me
Nor take me for a fool
Death claims us all
Soon I will fall
When my time is over
Bury me in clover.

Sarah Williams (13)
Fyling Hall School

The Seven Ages

Baby's crying, nappy is old,
Mother's too busy; the food grew some mould.
Baby's crying, her shoes are too tight,
But Daddy is coming to make it all right.

Now she's a toddler, the terrible twos,
She feels she can order *them* what to do.
Now she's a toddler, she's found some new friends,
But she claims there are monsters around every bend.

Her first day at school and she's acting all shy,
But her parents have told her that she mustn't cry.
Her first days at school and she's sick of it still,
But lessons now have to be part of her drill.

Her first term at college is really a treat,
She likes her course and a man named Pete!
Her last term at college has come to an end,
The doctor's degree means she's money to spend.

She's become engaged to a rich, powerful man,
But she called it off when she met a better man, Dan.
She's finally married and they've bought a new home,
But they left it to go on their honeymoon in Rome.

They now have nine children, they can barely cope,
Another's on the way so there is no hope.
Their family of children have grown up and left,
Now they are lonely and feel sad and bereft.

Her life has now ended but she doesn't mind,
She has no regrets; she's been treated kind.
Her life has now ended so her family mourn,
But her seventeenth grandchild was born at dawn.

Jennifer Maxfield (12)
Fyling Hall School

Blitz

Hazy overcast smoke
before my eyes.
Buzzing planes
all over the sky.

Sweltering fires
dancing all day.
People dying in the streets
in a really horrid way.

Burning bombs
explode with a bang.
Crashing down and down
to the ground.

Blaring sirens
in the street.
Waiting, waiting
Wait.

Deborah Boniface (11)
King James' School

Blind Girl's Questions

Mum, what colour's green?
Why is dirt considered obscene?
What's the sky and why is it blue?
What are clouds and what do they do?
Why are my eyes closed and others not?
What's a little? What's a lot?

Emma Kirk (12)
King James' School

Night Sky

No moon
Clouds move like dark fluffy pillows
Upon the midnight bed.

Crescent moon
The busy dizzy stars wander in the
midnight sky
Create a dream in my mind.

Half moon
Hanging in the east like half a
Wensleydale
It looks good enough to eat.

Full moon
The shadows creep across the sleepy sky
A golden coin in the water.

Johanna Hughes (11)
King James' School

Crossbow

The quarrel was cocked on the string,
A short iron blade on a long wooden shaft,
Soon the trigger was pulled,
And the bolt flew,
Scything and cutting the enemy ranks
before embedding itself in the mud.
The bowman smiled and shook his head,
Before falling to the ground,
Smote by a mighty sword,
Controlled by something greater.

Oliver Curl (11)
King James' School

Down In The Shelter

Down in the shelter
I hear the warden's call
Down in the shelter
I hear the bombs fall

Down in the shelter
I hear my dad's scream
Down in the shelter
I'm eating ice-cream

Down in the shelter
I see the searchlights bright and tall
Down in the shelter
I see the bombs fall

Down in the shelter
I hear the planes roar
Down in the shelter
I've got a wild boar.

Thomas Horsman (11)
King James' School

The Watching

Creeping through the trees
Pushing through the dead weeds,
I feel them, I see them
They are the past, the present, the future.
Again I run and the leader spots me
I'm being chased and fall
Falling, falling, falling.
They are watching me fall
They will watch forever.

Terri-Ann Hoggart (13)
Norton College

Feet

When you look around at people,
Then look at their feet,
Squared or long, short or strong,
You really can't compete.
You wonder why they're different,
You wonder why they're pink,
You wonder why they smell and well,
You think and think and think.
And if you really concentrate,
And look at all those lines,
You'll find for sure, that there's no cure,
For all those funny signs.
You use your feet an awful lot,
For walking round and standing,
For ballet dancing, jazz and prancing,
And for a safety landing.
On your feet, you'll probably wear,
Some of your socks and shoes,
Trainers, wellies or sandal jellies,
Whichever one you choose.
Your toenails can be painted pink,
Purple, green or blue,
Yellow or clear, red or a smear,
The choice is up to you.
Feet are really funny things,
If you think of it in a way,
They'll never change or be exchanged,
Not next year, tomorrow, today.

Sarah Hansen (13)
Norton College

DRAGONS

Where have all the dragons gone?
The ones within the story books,
that live in a world of castles and kings
and knights in shining armour?
Are they hiding in caves so deep
or flown away on luminous wings?

What has happened to the fire-breathing creatures,
with their scaly skin and great clawed feet?
Are they prowling the forests
or high in the mountains of some faraway country?

Where have all the dragons gone?
Were they ever really real or just another
myth?

Stacey Dunn (11)
Norton College

AFRICA CAME TO MY BEDROOM

As the letter box clinkered open and shut,
I rose from my bed all fezzerwazled,
I had just returned from Africa - where all my dreams begin.
At first I thought I saw monkeys swinging on my wardrobe,
They were all jifflefrumped, swaying from corner to corner,
Then I saw an elephant blugreniking on my window sill.
Behind the elephant was a filocering sunrise like never seen before.
Next I saw giraffes liloping around my shelf,
Hifforacing lions perched at the end of my bed were scary
At first but were all frizzgrupinging after.
I opened my eyes and everything melted,
'Goodbye Africa - see you tonight.'

Tessa Wain (11)
Norton College

Animals

Animals are big and small,
Some are tiny, some are tall,
Some are fat, some are thin,
Some have fur, some just skin.

All animals are so sweet,
Some eat veggies, some eat meat,
Everywhere you'll find some,
Tell them to and they will come,
Animals are very fun.

Animals are good friends,
They wait for you till school ends,
They lie asleep in their beds,
Rest down their little heads.

Briony McIlroy (12)
Norton College

Fantastic Football

Crazy corners
Great goals
Perfect players
Bouncing balls
Lively Liverpool
Man-U maniacs
Lazy Leicester
Baffled Bradford
Ragey Rangers
Nasty Newcastle
Frantic free kicks
Patient penalties
Hectic headers.

Helen Hepton (11)
Norton College

My Best Friends

First of all there's Terri,
She's a bit wacky
And slightly insane,
She never stops talking
Over again.

Then there's Sarah B,
When your life's a mess
She will always be there,
When you're thinking about boys
Or tearing out your hair.

Next there is Becky,
She's a right laugh,
She's always messing around,
Forever being daft
Acting the clown.

Then there is Sarah H,
She's always giggling
And talking at school,
She's an excellent friend,
She's really cool.

Next there's Alex,
She lives in my village,
I've known her for years,
When I am sad,
I know that she cares.

My friends are the best you can get,
I'd be nothing without them.

Friends are forever.

Sarah Carpenter (12)
Norton College

Perfect Pets

Cool cats,
Soft as mats.
Sweet dogs,
Better than hogs.
Spinning spiders,
Good hiders.
Helpful hamsters,
Perfect prancers.
Cute pigs,
Eat figs.
Soft cow,
To eat now.
Fat sow,
Eats chow.
Pretty rabbits,
Little grab-its.

Katie Townsend (11)
Norton College

Sea Life

Seals live in the sea
They swim and play like you and me.
Their babies are furry, cuddly and cute,
So why do people wear their skin for a suit?

Jenny Bonello (11)
Norton College

My Best Mate

My best mate,
there is no other.
We tell jokes,
and laugh at each other.

In class we laugh,
we never concentrate.
We are always messin',
me and my best mate.

We care for each other,
and share all we have,
she is truly the
bestest mate
I've ever had.

Rebecca Fox (12)
Norton College

Money

Money, money, money, can buy you pearls and jewels
and indoor swimming pools.
It can make you happy, it can make you sad.
It can make you good, it can make you bad.

Money, money, money is really cool!
Get some for yourself, don't be a fool!
But how do you get this money, we ask ourselves?
It's really simple, all you have to do is work and earn some money,
and if you're too lazy to go to work,
then you shall miss out on the pleasure of money.

David Stier (11)
Norton College

Day Of The Bomb

Memories from 'the day',
Of hurting souls and
Killing hearts . . .

People running everywhere,
From fear and disaster.
Fire!
Metal debris, stones.
Shock and injured people.

Explosions crying through the air.
Silence tries to suffocate,
But screaming breaks the spell,
As a small child cries loud tears.

Running to the school gates,
In panic and confusion.
Hoping that my child is there,
Alive . . .

Wading through the hall of blood,
Ash sticking to my fingers.
Seeing my child lying there,
I break down and cry.

Sarah Waite (13)
Oaklands School

I Look At The Sun

I look at the sun
With you and me together
Forever we'll stay.

Stacey Depa (12)
Oaklands School

Please Be My Girlfriend?

Please be my girlfriend
I'll do anything you want
I really am in love with you
I really am content.

Please be my girlfriend
I'll love you every day
I remember when we were kids
We used to laugh and play
I really think you're quite okay.

She gave me a smile
Then turned away
And went to another boy
She says
'Please be my boyfriend
I'll do anything you want . . .'

Matthew Dennis (12)
Oaklands School

Haiku

Rolling in the mud
keeping cool in the hot sun
grunting with his snout.

The rain is pouring
drip . . . drop, the rain is gushing
drip . . . the rain has stopped.

Large, wide eyes staring
big, sharp teeth ready to bite
pouncing on his prey.

Katie Carr (13)
Oaklands School

Me

K ind to other people,
A rtistic and poetic,
T he one and only,
H as three sisters,
L ives on Danebury Drive,
E ats all her lunch,
E ight years old is my little sister,
N ever gives up on her work.

I ngleward is our house,
N ever is mean or unkind,
G uitar is what I play,
L ove '5ive' the pop band,
E ggy bread is yummy,
B rings love and joy,
Y ork is where I live.

Kathleen Ingleby (12)
Oaklands School

Sunshine

The sun shines like the eye of heaven,
it opens up with the sound of a nightingale
and then closes again.
It's a beam of hope and inspiration,
and brightens up the morning sky.
It slices through the curtain of darkness with
its blinding ray,
it shines through the shield of water
and forms a pattern like precious jewels in
the sky.

Amy Whaite (13)
Oaklands School

A Dark Beauty

Darkness is seen in many different ways
Not all are completely true
Some pull it round them like a cloak
To conceal themselves in the shadows

For some, darkness means death
Creeping up to take them in their sleep
They cower in fear
At what horrid things lurk in the creeping shadows

Others see through darkness
Just as if it were broad daylight
Dancing in the sky
For them, this is day, not night

Darkness takes on many forms
And comes at different times
It is seen by most as dull and black
But others appreciate its eerie beauty.

Chris Taylor (13)
Oaklands School

Danny

Danny is red
He's the winter
He's the outside
He's thunder and lightning
He's a pair of Doc Martins
He's a wooden chair
He's a scary horror film
He's a big pizza.

Karl Horton (12)
Oaklands School

Blue

I like blue, it's really cool
it's the colour of the tiles in the swimming pool
maybe the colour of a shiny blue door
yes, blue is the colour I really adore.
Blue delphiniums stand really tall
the deep blue pools of a waterfall
a common colour of many people's eyes
blue is my bed where I do lie.
Blue is the toy box out on the floor
blue is the jumper my brother wore
my mate's pencil case is shiny blue
sparkling blue is my nanna's loo.
Lots of things are the colour blue
I love blue, how about you?

James Glenton (13)
Oaklands School

The Sunset

Like an arrow piercing the sky,
The sunset pushes the clouds apart,
To reveal a perfect, round gold ball.

Its strong rays breaking through,
Shining down on the sleepy people below,
Making patterns with the light.

As colourful as a rainbow,
The sunset shines and glistens,
As if it were the reflection on a smooth, clear piece of ice.

Charlotte Hoque (13)
Oaklands School

Seasons

In spring, the flowers start to sprout,
Baby lambs and other animals are born.
Easter is in spring and it's a time of joy.

The summer sun boils night and day,
People go on holiday and eat ice-cream.
Summer is a time of happiness.

In autumn, trees lose their leaves,
Harvest is in cold autumn.
The nights get dark early.

Kids make snowmen and go snowballing.
Christmas is a time to remember.
New Year is the start of it all again.

Ross Etherington (12)
Oaklands School

The Volcano

The volcano screams and spits fire
Into all its surroundings below,
Like a ferocious bear,
It howls and shoots fireballs
High up in the air,
Luminous goo,
Invades the cities too.
A trail of boiling slime as
Red as blood hits the cities
With a thud.
A sheet of flaming lava as
Hot as a kiln leaves everything dead.
Death and destruction result in corruption.

Michael Aldred (13)
Oaklands School

The Day Of The Bomb!

Ruins of the people's homes
Reduced to nothing
But burnt bricks
And charred photos

All their memories
Melted away
From that explosion, that cold sad day

The explosion was deafening
Birds flew from trees
I heard a mother scream

They are all gone
No chance to run
No warning
All is gone, people mourning

Fire ball ripped through the streets
As fast as a bullet
From a gun

Twisted metal
Where cars once stood
Glass in the street
From the school windows

No screaming children
No having fun
All are gone
No chance to run

I am all alone
What have I done
I planted the bomb
So go, quick, run!

Clare Wilson (13)
Oaklands School

Haiku

My bed is cosy,
But my mum knocks on my door,
It's Monday again.

The weekend has gone,
It's school again tomorrow,
I might just be sick.

The robins are singing,
High up in their little nests,
It makes me happy.

The sun has gone down,
The stars appear dancing
In the pitch black night.

I am in my shorts,
It's summer again today,
But now it's raining.

Sarah Watling (12)
Oaklands School

Football

At the football pitch
the ball rolls along the ground and stops
in the back of the net.

Martin Coulson (13)
Oaklands School

The Owl

Big eyes in the dark,
He flies off and aims at his prey,
Right on target, yes.

Kirsty Jackson (12)
Oaklands School

Haiku

I looked at the sky
The stars glistened like diamonds
They lit up the sky.

Jeremy Nicholson (12)
Oaklands School

The Dog

The dog is waiting
In the kennel with a bone
Waiting for a walk.

Ben Cairns (12)
Oaklands School

Autumn

In the cold dark street
Leaves are falling down from trees
Autumn is coming.

Becky Clayton (13)
Oaklands School

Titanic

In the Atlantic,
Scared people scream with terror,
The Titanic sinks.

Daniel Bettley (12)
Oaklands School

My Brother

Ryan is my brother
He was like a ray of sunshine
To my mother.

He is still my brother
But not quite so innocent
To my mother.

He's the baby of the house
And is as happy as a bee
He is like a flower
To my mother.

He is now growing up
And changing emotions all the time
But he is always happy
To my mother.

I love my brother
And the other one or two
They're still rays of sunshine
To my mother.

AnneMarie Howarth (13)
Oaklands School

Summer

Lying on the beach,
Waves crashing against the rocks,
Bright sun shining down.

Becky Robb (12)
Oaklands School

The Grandfather Clock

Like the marching of an army goes the
Tick, tock, tick, tock
Ding, ding, ding, ding
Goes the song of the grandfather clock.

Like a leopard
It just sits and waits
For the right moment
To pounce or chime.

Every hour it chimes
Without fail
Its song as graceful
As a whale.

Paul Jones (13)
Oaklands School

Tornado Poem

Round and round he goes,
Where he moves nobody knows,
He spins and spins like a tumble dryer.
A disaster setting the town on fire,
Leaving a trail behind,
He almost always wins,
He spins around,
Making an almighty, roaring sound,
Destroying everything.
He eventually storms away,
Like a spoilt child,
To come back and terrorise
Another day.

Chris Steggall (14)
Oaklands School

WAR

I look around and can see dead bodies
lying on the floor
like a heap of rag dolls,
their souls shattered by bullet and knife wounds.

In the distance there are remains of
buildings, like Lego buildings scattered by a child.

The sound of children crying, because of the
death of their loved ones and the cries from
the injured victims
echo through the town, like cries from cattle waiting
for the slaughter.

Scattered around me like discarded bird food are
my family, killed by the shooting.

The pain shoots through me like an arrow through
my heart as I sit at the feet of my dead mother.

I am trying to push the fact out of my head that I
am going to spend the rest of my life as an orphan,
in a partially knocked down old children's home
away from my remaining belongings and friends.

This war has hit us like a bomb exploding on the Earth,
destroying everything in its path.

When will it end?

Vicki Jackson (13)
Oaklands School

Like Pieces Of Pottery

Peace on Earth
Like a mirror image of an idealistic world
Shattered into a million pieces
Each individual, with its own views
Never to be placed back together
Peace on Earth existed no more.

War is raging deep within the hearts of the countries
The conflict is a ruthless monster, destroying people's lives, draining
Them of their hopes and desires.

People are enduring great suffering
Which will scar them for life
Permanent images of horror will be in their minds
The gun shots sounding like anguished screams.

Families suffering with the loss of loved ones
The throbbing pain of emptiness is unbearable
Trying to bury their grief and anguish
Covering it over with a masked smile.

The war has ended
Peace has been declared
It was as if nothing ever happened
Like it was just a dream.

People are china dolls, fragile and delicate
Trying to rebuild their lives
Putting it back to together, piece by piece
Just like pieces of pottery.

Rachel Pickering (14)
Oaklands School

Rivers

When a river flows downstream
Large, wide and ageless,
It wanders lazily, slow and bold

Peaceful, calm and dependable
It meanders round and round
Old fishermen gather
To see the glorious sight

Rushing, gushing, splashing around
What once was a peaceful river
Is now filled with rage

Shouting, bellowing, screaming
This huge river of terror
Speeding like a train

It races down the train track
Faster than a car
At last it begins to slow,
Slower, slower

It spreads out into the deep, blue ocean
Calm at last again
The journey has ended
And peace begins once more.

Peter Henderson (13)
Oaklands School

The Day Of The Bomb!

The world felt empty,
There wasn't a sound,
I awoke and saw plenty,
Of bodies around.
That was the day of the bomb!

Devastation lay around us all
All except from one
The body laid there silent and still,
That was the day of the bomb!

He lay there motionless on the cold wet floor,
With no expression on his face.
His eyes show fear and so much sadness,
I sit there in despair and disgrace.
That was the day of the bomb!

My son is dying
But no one comes to help
We wait for hours
And time is ticking away.
That was the day of the bomb!

My son is now dead
On the day of the bomb.
Why?

Emma Gill (13)
Oaklands School

The Sunflower

S itting in a garden, standing high,
U nder the cotton bud clouds in the sky,
N ever before have I seen such a flower so
colourful, so beautiful, so full of power.
F lowers small, flowers young, look up to
the towering tall stalk with a sun.
L ike a brush its stalk is prickly and rough,
O ften visited by the odd bumblebee or bird.
W inds knock the butter like petals from its head,
they fall gently to the flower bed.
E very time I see black clouds, like charcoal,
I think please don't let it tumble down.
R ainbows shine across the sky, bringing
showers to warm all the flowers.

Samantha Dykes (13)
Oaklands School

Daffodils

A host of radiant daffodils
Swaying in the dancing summer breeze
Cups of golden honey syrup
Inside soft, silken, sunkissed saffron.

A sea of molten gold
Gleaming in the blazing flame
Roaring with their lavish bronze tongues
Shimmering, shining, subtly standing.

Leah Blades (13)
Oaklands School

A Storm

A storm is coming,
It's starting to rain,
The wind is strong and the sky is grey.

A storm is so powerful, it can drag you away,
Litter is flying everywhere,
Trees are bending like soft rubber.

A storm is frightful,
Rain is getting heavier like tap water,
The wind is pushing everything out of sight.

The plate in the sky stands still,
The rain slows down and the wind stops talking,
Silence stalks the streets,
Everything is destroyed.

Gemma Kersey (13)
Oaklands School

John

John is a red heart
He is a hot summer's day
In school
He is sunny.
A school uniform
A bed
He is a comedy show
A rich and crispy apple.

Victoria Brooke (12)
Oaklands School

TEARS

Droplets like pearls,
Cascade down the peach surface,
Falling like rain,
Splashing onto the floor
Wiped away with the crisp tissue,
Discarded without a thought.
Salty like the sea,
Floating on your tongue,
Screwing your face up,
Eyes are empty,
All the tears have run away.

Until next time.

Julie Bray (14)
Oaklands School

MICHAEL OWEN

Michael Owen is green
He is the summertime
In a football stadium
He is hot.
A football player short
A sub bench
Michael Owens soccer training
Bananas before match.

Mark Powell (12)
Oaklands School

The Ingredients Of A Storm

For the perfect storm you need,
Thunder that explodes like atom bombs
And adds music to its beat.

Then add some lightning like volcanoes
And when bubbling, spread lava across the night sky,
Sending light through its fingertips.

After that, add a dark sky overcast with sorrow,
Which becomes bright and angry
When lit with a match.

And last of all, add a large sky
Because without it,
It would strike the Earth like an army in battle
And instead of leaving a memory of fireworks,
It would leave sorrow and hurt.

Samantha Robinson (13)
Oaklands School

An Ambulance Man

An ambulance man is green
He is wintertime
In a hospital
He is snowy.
He is a pair of overalls
He is a bed
An ambulance man is casualty
He's cheeseburger and chips.

Michael Jones (12)
Oaklands School

The Day Of The Bomb

I crawl, climb and clamber
Around in death's rubble
Pulse pounding, head hurting
Is he alive or is he dead?

A hand, a red shirt
But nothing just rubble.

Hey you!
I ran, stumbled, tripped and fell
Chasing a lost cause
It was not him
Somewhere inside I knew he had been consumed in death's blast.
I stagger towards my mind's hallucination.

I drop to my knees and weep and pray
I will find him.

James Agar (13)
Oaklands School

Alien

An alien is gold
It is autumn
In a pod
It is a thunderstorm,
An alien is a uniform
It is an advert
A squid in paella
A soft cushion.

Jason Smith (11)
Oaklands School

Love

Love is like a red, red rose
Wilting in the sun
But when I see your smile and face
I know mine's not that one.
My heart is lost upon misty clouds
Trying to find its way to you
To tell you darling my love for
You is true.
Your eyes like stars lightning up the sky.
Your lips like satin, oh for
Them I'd die.
So can we dance with
The stars under
A cosy
Blanket of
Night.

Kayleigh Reintoul (13)
Oaklands School

A Fisherman On The Riverbank

A fisherman is green
He is the summer, hot and sweaty
On a river bank
It is cool today
He is a rod, reeling them in
His posture is a chair
He is a fishing show
And likes nice fried mackerel.

Christopher Newnham (11)
Oaklands School

A Witch

A witch is black,
She is winter,
In a cold, gloomy castle,
She is thunder and lightning,
A witch is a black hat,
A black cauldron,
She is an advert,
She is a chicken curry.

Sarah Walker (11)
Oaklands School

Amy

Amy is red,
She is the autumn,
In her bedroom,
She is blustery,
Amy is a track suit,
A long sofa in a house,
She is Eastenders,
A big sweet fanatic.

Jenna King (11)
Oaklands School

Clouds

Abstract shapes of cotton wool,
Drift across the sky,
Towering above
Like huge snow-topped mountains
No care in the world
Just to expand and move on.

Come dark
And the white wonder turns to a
Mysterious pool of water,
Looming over everything
Casting an eerie darkness
Before it releases its curtains of hope.

Marie Walker (13)
Oaklands School

A Witch

A witch is black,
A witch is the winter,
In a dark cave.
She is riding in a storm.
A witch is wearing a long black cape.
A witch is a blow up chair in the shape of a spider.
A witch is a Hallowe'en advert.
She is a pair of frog's legs.

Hayleigh Reynolds (11)
Oaklands School

Leeds

Leeds are white,
In the football season,
In a stadium,
On rainy days,
Football socks,
Chairs for the crowd.
Channel Five, the footy channel,
Watch it whilst eating burgers.

David Clayton (11)
Oaklands School

Secrets

You led me to believe life was a bed of roses
With each pretty rose smelling sweetly
And their velvet petals embracing my soul.

But as lightning struck it sparked a fire
And lit up your eyes with fireworks
A burning secret hidden inside of you.

So I shed my cocoon of safety
And entered the world of the unknown
To find you hidden behind the clouds that held
Deep dark secrets.

Was I to look past their shadows of evil
And love you for who you are?
Or choose to disown you for who you were?

Kirsten Duffill (13)
Oaklands School

Santa Claus

Santa Claus is red
He is the winter
And is in his sledge.
He is snowy
Santa is in his red Santa suit.
A red velvet sofa is his sledge.
He is a Santa movie,
A crispy roast turkey.

Chris Bell (11)
Oaklands School

Autumn

Children wander aimlessly back to school,
Saddened at the end of the summer holidays,
The autumn term has begun.

The cloak of darkness now falls earlier than before,
The temperature gets colder, a nasty bite
And the wind howls through the trees like wolves.

Parachutes fall to the Earth from the trees above,
They turn red, yellow, orange and brown
And crunch underfoot like an apple being bitten.

Animals hoard up food for the cold winter months,
Before drifting to sleep.

Pomegranates come into season with their spiky hair style,
Small boys play with fruits of the horse chestnut.
This is autumn.

Matthew Anderson (13)
Oaklands School

Chelsea Player

He is summer,
He is blue,
He plays at Stamford Bridge,
He is thundery,
He wears a Chelsea kit,
He is a strong table,
He is Match of the Day,
He is steak and chips.

Ben Parker (11)
Oaklands School

Like Roaring Animals . . .

Like roaring animals
Red with anger
Lit up with fury
Trying to win a cup of gold
As bright as the sun
Racing round a figure of eight
Track of brown
Dots of coloured metal machines
Or wreckage and fire
Like a herd of wild bulls.

Zooming on a sea of dust
Furiously burning,
Crashing,
Flying into a spin
Landing upside down
Over a lake of yellow powder
The animals compete
To be first to see
The chequered flag.

As the sun moves gently
Across the sky
The dust settles
The fires end,
The noise stops
Everything is silent
On the racetrack.

Joe Tavener (13)
Oaklands School

In A Dream

The sun was setting in the east,
It was ninety degrees to say the least!
Snow was falling in the sky,
Do not ask me how, when or why?

It fell and fell for forty days,
Suddenly the fire set the house ablaze!
The flames climbed higher and higher,
Soon there was a great fire.

It melted the snow on the streets and cars.
Soon the water was higher than our house,
Much higher by far!

We sailed away in cardboard boxes,
We were stopped by hairless foxes.
They growled and showed their teeth,
Then they said 'What lovely things to eat!'

They took us to higher ground
And said to their friends, 'Look what we found!'
We climbed in a boat,
Then were tied up with strong rope.

I woke up scared and frightened,
So startled, my fists were tightened!
Mum walked up with a smile that was keen,
'Don't worry, you were in a dream!'

Heather Biddlecomb (12)
Queen Ethelburga's College

CANDLELIGHT

Candlelight,
Candlelight,
Burning bright,
Paint a picture of what happened this night.
Was it romance?
Was it violence?
Was it silence?
Was it love?
Was it hate?
Was it friendship?
Was it fate?
Whichever candlelight,
Paint a picture of what happened this night.

Katie Ewin (11)
Queen Ethelburga's College

FIRE

The sun beat down on an arid landscape
Animals burrowed hiding,
From its burning heat.
The man and his ox, turned
Walked up the track
To shelter under the straw covered veranda.

It can be a great tidal wave of
Flickering light, intense oppressive heat
Consuming everything in its path.
A fire breathing dragon
Men ran out, to quench its thirst
To no avail.

As the sun rose, over great plains,
It revealed a charred landscape
Devoid of life, abandoned
Bucket, erratic in the desert.
Preparing for a day in the
Soaring heat from the sun.

Alexandra Wrightson (15)
Queen Ethelburga's College

It Wasn't His Fault!

It wasn't the spider's fault that the fly died
It wasn't his fault at all!
If the fly hadn't been skydiving at the time
He wouldn't have taken the fall.

You see that stupid old fly fell into the web
And ruined poor spider's home
He even ruined the garden too
Including the garden gnome.

So don't go blaming poor spider.
I told you it wasn't his fault
That stupid old fly
Deserved to die
(But I'll tell you,
Fly would have had severe internal injuries
If spider hadn't have helped him out!)

Abbey Sykes (11)
Queen Ethelburga's College

The Bully

A new boy came to look round school yesterday,
He had a lot of cheek,
We had a spelling test,
He looked at mine to cheat.

I had to tell the teacher,
He pulled a face at me,
Unfortunately the teacher turned round to the
Blackboard
And I'm afraid did not see.

Luckily I don't think he's coming to this school,
For he hated me,
I think the teacher's glad,
Well I am totally!

Nina Hayes (11)
Queen Ethelburga's College

The Ring

The ring is a symbol
So round and unique
It symbolises love
And eternity.

For some it is an accessory
Bought cheap, at a local store
For others it was given
By a loved one.

Some people wear theirs
Forever until they die
Some wear it when they want,
Others keep it in the presentation box.

As I stare at this ring
Wondering whose fingers it has seen,
Wondering whose lives it
Has lived with.

I slip the ring on my finger
And live my life with it.

Amy Martin (15)
Queen Ethelburga's College

The Dust Man

He is there behind the curtains,
Through the shadows he does creep,
He goes dancing in the moonlight,
When you're trying to get to sleep.

And although you cannot see him,
You know that he is there,
'Cause of the shimmering sound the dust makes,
When it goes flying through the air.

He comes tiptoeing to your bedside,
Then throws dust into your eyes
And the feeling is amazing,
Because he gets you by surprise.

You get a dizzy feeling
And a tingling in your brain,
Your awareness he is stealing,
When you catch the Dreamtown train.

Lucy Chambers (12)
Queen Ethelburga's College

WAITING

We sit there waiting, nothing else just waiting,
Occasionally there's a slight disturbance,
A thought, an idea, a flash of inspiration,
But then it goes and we're back to waiting.

It's getting later now, darkness is drawing in,
We start to panic,
'What have we done, except waiting and merely existing?'
In moments of desperation we try telling
Ourselves we've done something, something
Important that makes us different.
Then we realise we're all just the same and
We wait some more.

One of us stirs,
'That's it, I'm not going to just sit around like
I have been doing, I'm going to do something.'
He attempts to stand but suddenly stops,
Too scared to be the first.
He slips back into his familiar position thinking to himself
'I'll wait for someone else to go first, then I'll follow.'
That someone never comes.
We all just wait.

Life is there for living, not just mere existence.
Don't wait for it to grab you, you've got to grab it with both hands.
Make sure you're living your life to the max!

Charlotte Mason (15)
Ripon Grammar School

It's Love But Remember That

Love is waiting patiently by the garden gate,
Delight if I'm early, despair if I'm late
Favourite fodder flattening the table,
Stuffing myself, telling her about my day, if I am able.
Love is naked pride at my attainment,
Corner eye crystal dewdrops, doting, devoted adornment.
That staunch, steadfast smile, that look of unconditional,
bottomless loving,
Making it obvious so that I'm always knowing.

Love is going shopping,
Painfully pounding streets until she's dropping.
Returning home, aching, singing 'Mochyn du' in Welsh harmony,
Making mystical, magical days momentous for me.
Love is the childhood stories. Petunia the pig, Fox the horse,
Old Don the sheep dog painted white without remorse.
Nelly's mud squelching, bellowing, heavy panting,
Udders full, sideways swish swoshing, pummelling.

Love is also the saying of 'no'
'You're out of line.' 'You must not do.'
No raising of voice, no tempers blazing,
Just a quiet word. Love remains in the gazing.
Love is the discreet, smile making, diminishing of pain,
Telling me white lies, those distracting diversions again and again.
The cushioning, the caressing, the cosseting, the consoling.
Constant cherishment - it's not confusing.

It's love - but remember that this love makes one wise,
To the plight of others, to hear their cries.
Some have their right to a mother's love aborted,
By death, tragic accidents, political systems all distorted.
To those who are suffering from such a plight,
We must show we truly care - it's only right.

Ruth Mitchell (11)
Ripon Grammar School

THE INTERNET

Surf,
Shop,
Find out news,
Watch the eclipse,
Watch TV.

Find a friend,
E-mail,
Chat,
Play multiplayer mode,
On games,
Use it well.

Get info,
Use it for,
School,
Meet your friends,

But,
Above all,
Have fun!

Nat Nabarro (11)
Ripon Grammar School

IT ISN'T MY FAULT

It isn't my fault that the dog can't open doors
And it has a tendency to wee on the floor.

It wasn't my fault that I hit Lisa's head
You know I've got a temper when I get woken from my bed.

It isn't my fault that my chores are not done
I wanted to play outside and chores are no fun.

It isn't my fault that in all of my school work there's a fault,
When will you realise that . . .
It isn't my fault!

Nicky Maguire (11)
Ripon Grammar School

Wonderful Potion

Mix up a wonderful potion
Throw where there is commotion
Tell everyone about this great lotion
Get rid of dirty pollution.

Mix up a wonderful potion
Throw it where there is commotion
Then tell everyone about this great lotion
Get rid of dirty pollution
Let everybody use this solution
No war only peace
Oh what a potion.

Get set to make your paces
Use the potion to rid of the racist
Get rid of upset faces
By making wonderful places
Let everybody use this solution
No war only peace
Oh what a potion.

Jason Metcalfe (11)
Ripon Grammar School

The Rules Of The World

Cars are dirty,
Ships spill oil,
Trucks pollute the sky and soil.

Dodo gone,
Tamarin on the way,
They have no words left to say.

Goodbye to the rainforest,
Adios to the world in the sea,
Who do you really want to be?

A doctor, a dentist, that's just fine,
Don't be a polluter or you're no friend of mine!

Ride bicycles to school each day,
Don't say bye to the world today.

The Snow Leopard says goodbye to his wife,
Because the way he's going, it's the end of his life.

Should it not be the other way around?
The Snow Leopard snug and safe and sound,
With man in the trees struggling along,
Knowing that his life won't last that long.

Think about it the other way around,
You're not so happy and glad are you?
The world will turn bad some day,
Not a word left for anyone to say!

Megan Rex (11)
Ripon Grammar School

Reflections Of The Year

Winter is snow and frosty mornings,
Winter is floods and gale warnings,
Winter is a time to stay at home,
Winter is a time not to be alone.
Winter is cold and white and still
And long dripping icicles hang off the window sill.

Spring is the time when flowers come,
Spring is a time of laughter and fun.
Spring is when eggs hatch into birds,
Spring is a time often put into words.
Spring is the time when life's at its best,
When children play and never rest.

Summer is when the light never ends,
Summer is happiness, freedom and friends.
Summer is pleasure and summer is smiles
And picnicking, having walked long miles.
Summer is when we all go abroad,
To Disneyland or the Norwegian fjords.

Autumn is when the weather gets colder
And the leaves turn gold, getting older and older.
Autumn is when the horse chestnuts fall
And people are out there, finding them all.
Autumn is when children go back to school
And once again, the teachers rule!

Anna Rutter (11)
Ripon Grammar School

If I Had One Wish

If I had one wish I could get a cat
A computer, a telly or even a rat,
A horse, a dress or those CD's
A double bed or chips for my tea.

If I had one wish I could have chocolate bars
A bag of sweets or drives in flashy cars
A snake, blonde hair or the sunshine
A holiday or a coat with a fleecy line.

If I had one wish I could have a zoo
An art kit, a painting set for me to do
A football, a yo-yo or even money
A trip to see Boyzone or a pot of honey.

If I had one wish I could become smart
A cow, Alan Shearer or even a jam tart
A pop star, a pencil or even a glue stick
A piece of cheese, a troll or really thick.

If I had one wish I know what I'd choose
A thing worth more than a pair of new shoes
A thing that will last forever and ever
Happiness, happiness, sadness never!

Lauren Moffat (11)
Ripon Grammar School

The Fridge

I wanted a drink
So I went to our big fridge,
And I froze to death.

Peter Ransome (13)
Ripon Grammar School

THE PRIMARY COLOURS

Red is the colour of danger,
Like being approached by a tall, dark stranger.
Red is a colour saying stop
And the colour of a strawberry lollipop.
Red is the colour of anger and rage
And roses on mid summer days.
Red is fuming and hot,
Like a heated cooking pot.
Red is . . .

Blue is the colour of sadness
And can drive you to madness.
Blue is the colour of the ocean
And a shining new locomotion.
Blue is the colour of the sky
And the bilberries you put in a pie.
Blue is when you're feeling lonely
And you feel it's you only.
Blue is . . .

Yellow is the colour of smiles
And the sun setting for miles.
Yellow makes you feel warm,
When the sun is rising at dawn.
Yellow is the brick road,
That you travel with your load.
Yellow is a banana skin
That you pick up and throw in the bin.
Yellow is . . .

Ben McDonald (11)
Ripon Grammar School

Save The Animals

Giant pandas,
Tiny quails,
Huge rhinos,
Humpback whales,
Save the animals.
Save the world.

Tall, tall trees,
Open spaces,
Sandy deserts,
Bushy green places,
Save the animals.
Save the world.

Asian elephants,
Large green frogs,
Clever cats,
Wise old dogs,
Save the animals.
Save the world.

Emma McTague (11)
Ripon Grammar School

Contrasts

Darkness all around me,
Day is now all gone;
Bright stars twinkle above me,
Cats come out to hunt.
Dogs then start to howl
And lights start coming on,
The stars are just clouds now
And the moon is now the sun.

The waves lap up around me,
They freeze my body and soul;
I'll never know what's below me,
For the water's as deep as my home;
But the sand is a golden yellow,
It blows in the wind through my hair,
It sticks to my body and scratches me,
But there's no need to be scared.

Laura Mundy (12)
Ripon Grammar School

MATHEMATICS!

Maths! It's a subject of disaster,
All children have to learn it,
It drives the brain to suicide
I'd really like to burn it.

In the USA they call it Math,
It's shorter and perhaps more easy
But here it's mathematics and
It leaves me hot and sneezy.

I set about it with great gusto
But soon feel quite frustrated,
I think I'll use my calculator
As all these problems must go.

Decimal, percentage and fraction,
Are very hard to master,
I'll really have to speed my actions
And move a fraction faster.

But still I'll have to point out
I'll never really like it!

Catherine Lilley (12)
Ripon Grammar School

SHELTER OF THE NIGHT

I went out at the dead of the night,
Walked in the world and was free,
Free from my sorrows,
Free from my fears,
Alone with my thoughts and me.

In a world of my own I wandered,
Over moss carpeted moors,
The moon as my guide,
To show me the way,
Surrounded by damp heather floors.

I strolled along, not a care in the world,
The smells of the night filled the air,
The soft sweet breeze,
Rustled through the trees,
Nothing could disturb me there.

The moon was fading, the sun shimmered through,
Dawn was breaking too fast,
Sorrows seemed to beckon,
Fears loomed overhead,
How long 'til the moon its kind shadows will cast?

Susie Metcalfe (11)
Ripon Grammar School

A BOY'S PERFECT CHRISTMAS

I wake up and run into the front room
I automatically look under the tree.
A pile of presents, just for me,
I rip them all open and low and behold
There is that Game Boy I yearned to hold.

I play on it for hours on end
But it eventually drives me up the bend
It is now under my bed
I think I'll start collecting stamps instead.

Kate Markham (11)
Ripon Grammar School

A Spring

A spring
Is like a
Tornado,
Twisting
Round and round.

A spring
Is like a
Marathon
Stretching
Really long.

A spring
Is like a
Rope
Stretching which
Is really very long.

A spring
Is stretchy
Very
Very
Stretchy!

Jonathan Park (11)
Ripon Grammar School

The Magic Man

His body is like a systematic machine.
He is a great lover of all things
And moonlit nights, spent drinking wine and dancing.
His eyes are like fire, burning with the fury of hell,
His breath, a cool breeze on a midsummer's eve
Beauty his life;
To be without beauty is to him like a cruel and twisted death.
His touch is like a butterfly;
A majestic animal;
His footsteps like music;
Echoing eternal
His mind whispers a song never played.
The darkest secrets of mankind are stored in his memories;
So complex, like a web, a network, made by the fabric of time.
Space is his territory, never-ending, never changing
Mystery surrounds him; with the future in his palm.
The past is an old book, read again and again
through the dimensions.
The master of time: The Magic Man.

Luke Symonds (13)
Ripon Grammar School

Love

Love is coming home from school,
Love is swimming in a pool,
Love is acting like a fool,
Love is . . .

Love is walking across a field,
Love is winning a silver shield,
Love is eating your favourite meal,
Love is . . .

Love is scoring the winning goal,
Love is watching a mare and foal,
Love is going into bat or bowl,
Love is . . .

Love is eating a large ice cream,
Love is dreaming up a dream,
Love is paddling in a stream,
Love is . . .

Sam Lord (11)
Ripon Grammar School

Look Inside You

Don't look into the mirror
Look inside you
To find out who you are.

Don't listen to what people say
They have no idea what you're like
Just listen to what's inside you.

People can make you feel insecure
Like you're not good enough for them
But it's they, who aren't good enough for you.

Fat, thin, ugly or pretty,
We all deserve a chance
Take it if you get it.

Don't look into the mirror
Look inside you
To find out who you are.

Elizabeth Needham (13)
Ripon Grammar School

MESSAGE CLEAR

                              Love?
      is
      i t   a
Wh i t   e
                          d   ove?
                      a
Hat   a
                d   ale
                      a
            word
              or   a
W   i   ll
   T is   all
W a   s   all
What is this word called Love?

Josh Moore (12)
Ripon Grammar School

FOOTBALL

F lying shots, raining in on goals,
O utstanding saves, skills and turns,
O ften goals are scored and crowds go wild,
T ieri Henri, just on, beats one man, beats two, shoots . . . it's a goal!
B oring sport, some people say,
A waste of time and money, someone remarked,
L ost again this week - not worth watching,
L eaving for home, the day is over.

Thomas May (11)
Ripon Grammar School

THE SCHOOL DAY

The bell rings
For the end of break
And I'm ill, I fake.

I tell my next teacher,
He sees if it's true
But he must be stupid, cause he says it too.

I go to reception
Covered in gloom
I tell her I'm ill, so she sends me to the sick room.

While I plot my revenge
I see her again
I miss the boy behind her and shout out *Miss Lane*.

As soon as I see him
I gasp in surprise
For he has a splinter stuck in his thighs.

Miss Lane gives me an essay
For shouting too loud
And after that, I don't feel very proud.

The boy sits beside me
And now I feel sick
'Cause at his scab, he starts to pick.

I reach for the bucket
And let it all out
In comes Miss Lane and she starts to shout . . .

'What are you doing?'
'I know you are ill'
'But if you're going to be sick, don't do it on Phil.'

Michael Holmes (11)
Ripon Grammar School

Night Is . . .

Night is silk and glitter,
Night is all of a jitter,
Night is flashing lights,
Night is rowdy fights.

Night is game shows on TV,
Night is pop songs on CD,
Night is the stars in the sky,
Night is the moon up high.

Night is crisp, white frost,
Night is animals lost,
Night is cold, wet rain,
Night is a cold window pane.

Night is a drink of hot milk,
Night is pyjamas made of silk,
Night is cosy in bed,
Night is dreams in your head . . .

Sally Netherwood (11)
Ripon Grammar School

The Ghost

Shadows creeping there
Psychedelic blacks and greys
Now forever gone.

Holly Johnson (12)
Ripon Grammar School

MESSAGE CLEAR

He   commands
                           past
                        the   future
    who   conquers
He   commands
           m   an
                               st   at   e
                  a   st   a   r
He   c   he   at   s
                      d   e   a   th
           m   a   ste   r
        o   f
           m   a   n
        command   conquer
h   o   u rs
            o   f
                               st on   e
He   c   an
          com   e t o   the   future
He   commands the past
He who commands th   e   future
He who commands the past conquers the   future.

Anna Lewicki (12)
Ripon Grammar School

STORM

Diamonds shatter flash,
Curling clouds and windows thrash,
Stars in heaven smash.

Zoe Green (12)
Ripon Grammar School

UNTITLED

No
o n e
know s
the
po t e n ti al
o f
the imagination
the imagination
is the
l i f e
is the
power
is
d ea th
Knowledge
is
al l
th a t
I
know
the imagination
is
al l
th a t
I
s e e
Knowledge is not nearly as powerful as the imagination.

Alex Nicolaides (12)
Ripon Grammar School

I Can't Write Poetry!

I fluked a test to a Grammar School
Where everyone writes poetry,
I told them I can't write poems
And who ever let me in must be a fool.

Every night I sit watching TV
While my mum writes my poems
And does the homework
For my sister and me.

My mum is always saying
When it comes to 'A levels'
To get me to do well
How much will she be paying?

Complaining to my mum
Are letters from my school
Asking why my work is a mess
And only half done.

I can't be asked to do my poetry
There's football, Game Boys, computers
Which are more interesting
Not to mention the old TV.

All over my books are C's, D's and E's.
Crosses but not ticks,
Which makes Mum
And teachers most displeased.

Harriet Hurrell (12)
Ripon Grammar School

A Nature's Force

Outside the trees all whisper
A darkness in the night
A shudder and a tremor
Shakes the good filled light.

The warm inside gets stronger
Hunch around the fireplace
A freezing cold is shattered
Fading into true disgrace.

A human would be foolish
To try curving nature's power,
An ignorance to mother earth,
At its most darkened hour.

You may think mud's a problem
A bit of heavy rain
You think that winds are whipping
It's all just one big pain.

Weather's a solid feeling
A wonderful, harsh revolution
The world takes on its own fight
Coming with its own solution.

Rosie O'Connell (12)
Ripon Grammar School

The Millennium

The Millennium Bug, it's not real
Are computers solid rock steel?
The end of the millennium is a scary thing
The world will end with an intergalactic ring.

The end of the millennium is a time to party,
People dress up and look rather tarty
Go out for a meal, do whatever's right
If you get really drunk don't get in a fight.

Harriet Johnson (12)
Ripon Grammar School

FACE IT, LIVE IT

F r e e
Your fears
F e e l
your dreams
fac e
you
Fac e u s
R e live
Your fears
Re live
yo ur dreams
I am
F i r e
Face u s
I am
a
dream
F e ars
Live your dreams
You ar e our dreams
Face your fears, live your dreams.

Fiona Mactaggart (12)
Ripon Grammar School

Dawn

All is still and dark,
Not a rustle.
Everywhere is deserted,
For the whole world sleeps.

The hills stand lonely,
All by itself,
So unimportant yet mysterious,
So ordinary in the distant view.

But as the darkness slowly lifts,
The world begins to stir.
The birds slowly waken,
To see the new day rise.

They look towards the hill,
Standing on its own.
Then out of the dark sky,
Comes a ray of pure bright light.

Just a ray at first,
But then beginning a circle,
It rises and rises in the sky,
Till at last it settles.

The circle of light is so wonderful,
Giving light to us all,
The sky becomes a sea of blue and orange,
The silent hill stands high.

The cockerel crows,
The world is awake,
Ready to begin once more,
The dawn has just broken and a new day is born.

Amy Rowlatt (12)
Ripon Grammar School

The Phrase Of Today For Tomorrow

li f e
is the future
live i t
l o v e i t
h a ve i t
forget
the past
for
I've the
future
live to the future
h a v e the future
Live life to the future, forget the past

Mathew Ankers (13)
Ripon Grammar School

Message Clear

M a n
n e
e
d
s
m a n
a
m a n
a l one
is n o.
M a n
No man is an island alone.

Stephen Nesbitt (12)
Ripon Grammar School

MESSAGE CLEAR

Lif e
I s a
Thrill
Wi th
A d venture
I n
Th e
Wi l d
Life is a d a re
A n d
F is h a re
Aw a re
Th a t
I t
I s
Sa d

W h en
I t
d I e
S
Li ve
A
F u
ll
Life
Life is a wild thrilling adventure.

Christopher Pemberton (12)
Ripon Grammar School

MESSAGE CLEAR (MY VERSION)

N e ve r
be
scared always be
brave
Don't li e
a b ou t
car r y
on be brave
n o t
a
b a b y
I
n e ed to
be brave
be c o o l
Don't be scared always be brave, live your life to the full.

Ally Jones (12)
Ripon Grammar School

MILLENNIUM ON THE MOON

I'd like to spend the millennium on the moon,
Then I can watch the world fall to its doom.
I don't want to spend the millennium at home,
I'd rather be spending it in the heat of Rome.
I don't want to spend the millennium at school,
Recapping 2000 years of history is cruel.
I'd rather not be on the Earth warm and snug,
'Cos you're all going to get hit by the Millennium Bug!

Pippa Hollins (12)
Ripon Grammar School

MILLENNIUM COUNTDOWN

10, 9, 8,
We countdown
7, 6, 5,
To the beginning of the millennium.

4 seconds to go
Bring out the pizza
Pepperoni, sausage,
Or even supreme.

3 seconds till the bell
Pour out the wine
Beer and all
For us to celebrate.

2 seconds
1 second
Yeah!
It's here!

Pop goes the wine
As everyone parties
Having a good time
And getting drunk on beer.

Now the partying
Is over,
We can go to bed
Happy we made it.

Nathaniel Nichols (12)
Ripon Grammar School

FORBIDDEN FUTURE

The future and all the millennium
Computers take over each day,
Silver's an every year fashion
The new age has come by the way.

Computer chips tidy our houses,
Holograms take over mail
Nearly every tiger is gone now
And what the heck is whale?

Hey let's go to the moon today
A return ticket's quite cheap
We'll see the Leaning Tower of Cheese
It is 3000 feet steep.

The world has changed since the year two K
We were nearly gone by World War 3
The space suit was last year's garbage
When you get to the moon you'll see.

The best holiday this year is Mars,
The biggest sights are at Uranus
We all live in a World of Robots
The 1990's are far behind us.

Goodbye to the past now,
Bye to the good old land,
It was gone in a wink of an eye
Say bye to hot air and sand.

No one lives on Earth now,
That place is dead and gone.
Everyone lives on the lunar surface
It's cold but we get along.

Harriet Scales (12)
Ripon Grammar School

Lost

To associate objects with desires.
Objects enhance such desires,
But also eliminate them.
Do we do it to remind ourselves?
Or to like the object more so it becomes our desires?
If the object was our desire
It would be easier to obtain.
Take light as an object to associate with good.
Stereotyped ways can lead to false pretences.
Darkness can be good
In darkness we sleep, therefore we dream.
Dreams are treasured and lead to desire!
We live in circles,
Knowing what we truly want
Is almost impossible to obtain.
That impossibility can be soothed,
Until we find what we are looking for.

Helen Webster (15)
Ripon Grammar School

I Can't Write Poetry

I can't write poetry even if I try
I come up with a lot of nonsense and it even makes me cry,
It takes me all day to even write a line,
I hope not being able to write poetry isn't a crime
Why oh why do we have to do
Poetry!

Nicola Stone (12)
Ripon Grammar School

Teabags And Coffee Grains

I get scorched by the red hot water,
Get squeezed by the silver spoon,
Get drank by the men and women
I will be in heaven soon.

I get bought from the supermarket,
I get scooped out of the pot,
Get attacked by the kettle water,
And drank while I'm hot.

I've made friends with my mate Coffee,
I've made friends with my mate Tea,
We get along fine now,
And coffee is rather like me!

Laura Koscik (12)
Ripon Grammar School

Elephant

Elephants are big
They're also very strong,
If you think I'm lying,
Then you are in the wrong.

They have a loud trumpet
They're also scared of mice,
But if you get deep inside
They really are quite nice.

Their favourite food is shrubs
But they also eat from trees.
They've got a tail at the other end
Used for swatting bees.

Richard Hebb (14)
Ripon Grammar School

Millennium And The New Year's Eve Before

People are excited
planning lots of parties
it's a new year
the same as every other one
its got a special name
so people are changing the prices
pubs are charging people to enter
and when they leave they can't remember.
New babies being born
they read it in the paper when to conceive!
Although it may be different on New Year's Eve
no one is going to be able to breathe.
It's gonna be so funny
but because it's still night-time
the hangovers are still to come.

Pauline Rudd (13)
Ripon Grammar School

The Owl

The soaring giant is in the sky,
His majestic body just sliding through the air
His pin point eyes can see a mouse from his path
High in the sky,
Then, in a second, he has swooped down and is back up
To a perch, with the mouse in his talons.

Rory Lippell (12)
Ripon Grammar School

She

She was nothing like the others,
She was alone all day and night.
She was twisted up with evil and hate
And confused between fear and spite.

She was abandoned as a baby
Been an orphan for fourteen odd years
She thinks about nothing but death and destruction
And evil is all that she hears.

The hate was burning her up inside
The hate for those people who left her
They made her an evil creation
And twisted up her mind forever.

She never had any friends at school,
So no one noticed when she was gone.
No one even questioned her absence
No one, absolutely no one.

Eventually people asked where she had gone
But the truth is, as you will see
Is that she is living inside some of us
It could be you, it could be me.

Claire Hinchcliffe (13)
Ripon Grammar School

The Mouse

The mouse was needed
On the biggest assignment;
To get the black cat.

James Rowbottom (12)
Ripon Grammar School

Millennium Fever

As we approach the year 2000
The world is full of change.
Our lives are run by computers
From work - to fun and games.

All the parties should be good,
Lots of food and champagne,
And when the stroke of midnight comes,
The world will be full of joy.

But there is a little consequence
That we cannot deny,
As we party until midnight
The Earth could simply die.

The Millennium Bug - rubbish!
Or so many people said.
But how can we be sure
Until all technology is dead.

But we must think on the bright side
Of all the fun to have,
We must not think of pain and sadness
But think of joy and love.

Lizzy Rose (13)
Ripon Grammar School

Teeth

After a hard day,
Pick up your toothbrush and clean.
Your teeth sparkle white.

Emily Twitchell (13)
Ripon Grammar School

Blue

Blue, the colour is so meaningless
Like a vast outstretching ocean,
It's clear but dull
No noise can be heard - silence,
It's bold like a cloudless sky.
No movement
It doesn't stretch but twists round square-cut corners
Blue songs,
A feeling of sadness,
So many emotions,
All mingled together
Trapped
By a blue mood.
Depression and sadness
Surrounded by guilt
Blue.
The spring-fresh smell
The sense of quietness
Loneliness
Alone is a world
A world full of blue
Nothing else
But blue.

Laura Hornsey (14)
Ripon Grammar School

Winter

I stole the trees leaves,
I cover the grass with snow,
Yet spring will catch me.

Jo Tarren (13)
Ripon Grammar School

Memories

The house was like an antique shop
He sat there in delight
Showing all the odds and ends
That we could see in sight.

The air was full of happiness
Never of sadness or gloom,
We were the little twinkling stars
And he was the bright shining moon.

We never seemed to tire of him,
Or come to that, get bored.
We were his ladies and gentlemen
And he was our Lord.

He was such a clever and happy man,
It was sad to see him go.
But we will always remember him,
For being jolly and not full of woe.

He is in our hearts forever,
Cocooned with all our love,
Because he belongs in heaven
With all the bright white doves.

Kathryn Hudson (14)
Ripon Grammar School

Imagination

The sky is purple,
The people are green and blue,
The animals red.

Lorraine Wright (13)
Ripon Grammar School

LIFE

Life begins when your eyes first open,
Life begins when your first words are spoken,
When your legs are strong
And you can't go wrong,
That's when life begins.

When you go to school
And you are taught your first rule,
If you get down to work
And do it well, you will get to drive a Merc,
That's when life begins.

When you get your first boyfriend,
You will wish it will never end
And when he finds another girl other than you,
You will cry but then you will find another boy too.

You will find a husband,
Who will be the man of your dreams,
You will end up getting married
And go to your wedding in a golden carriage.

You might live a life of happiness,
Or a life of misery,
But whatever happens in your life,
You must never give up.

You must live a life of courage,
Not a life of fear,
Face your problems,
Otherwise they will never go away.

Jessica Parkinson (13)
Ripon Grammar School

TIGER

Can you see the tiger
Hunting through the night?
Can you see the tiger pounce
Before the bird takes flight?

Can you hear the tiger
Growling at the tree?
Can you hear the tree's reply
That sets the tiger free?

I can see the tiger
Hunting through the night,
I can see the tiger pounce
Before the bird takes flight.

I can hear the tiger
Growling at the tree,
I can hear the tree's reply
That sets the tiger free.

I can also hear the tiger call
Before the hunter shoots him.
Then I hear the tiger fall
Then I hear nature call
Then I know
What the world has lost
To a money-hungry, heartless hunter.

Laura Robinson (13)
Ripon Grammar School

Why Oh Why?

Why oh why is this planet a mess
If you don't know, can't you guess?
Why are we killing off this place,
Can't someone get on the case?
Too many cars pollute the land,
From the polar ice to the desert sand.
It will kill more than an animal or tree
And they'll leave the problem to me.
The greenhouse gas is warming the Earth,
New York, Alaska, Hong Kong, Perth.
The warmth will change the world drastically
Changing many a plant and tree.
There's not enough resources for us to carry on,
Our comfy-like lifestyles may soon be gone.
The coal supply is running dry
So the end could be nigh.
More species of animals are becoming dead
Killed for their tusks, teeth or head.
Animal homes replaced by tar
That's just a passage for a car.
Stealing, murder, riots, war
Make me shout out 'Please - no more!'
Don't they realise they're killing the planet,
And that can't be good - can it?
But the ozone layer was about to go
So let that to you be a show,
Some things can be turned round
Then the answer will be found.

Andrew Mealor (13)
Ripon Grammar School

This Love

I want you all for myself,
Can't bear to see you with anyone else,
The feelings that I feel for you
Have and will always remain true.
Love is so good when there are two
People involved, just me and you.
I will never be free
Because you'll always be a part of me.
I wish that you were mine,
When I see you, my face shines,
It gives off the most radiant glow
Which through all my feelings show.
But when you're gone
The world goes wrong
And days and nights feel so long.
I hope that one of these days,
We can get it back, that way.
Please come back into my life again,
Not having you is driving me insane.
I hate this feeling
I sometimes think I'm dreaming
But I'm not,
I hate this pain I've got.
I had this love but now its gone
He'll always be my number one,
And when I see a pure white dove
It'll remind me of what used to be this love.

Rachel Moore (13)
Ripon Grammar School

FRIENDS

I used to know what it was like just to be alone,
I used to cry all the time, wishing I was at home,
But even at home I was still alone, thinking in my bed,
Why was I always alone - sometimes I wished I was dead.
It was not fair I had no friends, I looked at people having fun
I was really sad and I felt as if I was being burnt by the sun.
They laughed and even shouted at me all day long
Whatever they did, they did not care because they did not
think it was wrong.
But in the end I had a few friends who were being
nice to me,
I wasn't alone, I had some friends, from the lonely pit
I had been set free.
They laughed at my jokes and we all had fun.
Now that I'm happy I definitely know that from home
I'll never run.
We talk a lot and have the time of our lives now
I've got loads of friends - even more than twenty-five.
Now that I'm not alone it doesn't feel as if I'm trapped
in a load of nettles.
Now I'm very happy and I have learnt that my friends
are extremely special.

Lena Jawad (13)
Ripon Grammar School

THE LION

Eyes sharp, mouth wide
Running prey moves into sight
One quick thrust it's upon its prey
Eats it up without a trace

Philip Hardisty (14)
Ripon Grammar School

They All Lived Happily Ever After

Once upon a time
Lived a gorgeous princess who had a handsome
stalker who wanted her dead.
She lived in a castle on a council estate,
with her 47 stepsisters and hooligan mates.

Now one fine day she was spray-painting
a wall,
When her mate called Tracey gave her a call.
'Oi Cinderella, take a look at this,
that lad that you fancy is asking for a kiss!'

So darling Cinderella went to meet her
true love,
He gave her a slap then he gave her a hug.
It was love at first sight,
They were made for each other.

And they lived happily ever after with
one another.

Joanne Satariano (13)
Ripon Grammar School

Nature

Tiger in a wood surrounded by trees
Pig on a bridge over crystal water
Puffin on a rock against the sky
Sheep in a field eating green grass.

Black kitten in a kitchen playing with wool
Dolphins gliding in the turquoise seas
Eagles floating high in the hills
Goldfish in a tank surrounded by weed.

Seal on the white ice of the Arctic
Crab running along a sandy white beach
Cheetahs roaming the Kenyan plains
Rabbit's feet bang in danger.

Dodos long ago extinct
Camels walking in the desert
Monkeys swinging from tree to tree
Donkeys on a beach carrying children high
Fish swimming through the corals.

Kate Petty (14)
Ripon Grammar School

MURDER

Shaded by a curtain of streaked orange, the ape slouched in the nest
carefully created out of the forest's fresh foliage.
The hunter, who was disguised as part of the jungle in his khaki
uniform crouched in the undergrowth.
She reached up with a leathery hand, to pluck another fruit from the tree
she was nesting in.
He began to load his rifle with small shiny cartridges and scanned the
dense forest for orang-utans.
Her kind, almost human eyes, had now spotted the intruder, she shrank
into her nest slightly but continued to munch the nutritious fruit.
His eyes narrowed as he lifted the gun and prepared his aim.
The primate was still unaware of her almost certain fate.
The hunter squinted up at the sun, perfected his aim and pulled
the trigger.
The orang-utan met the cold stare of her killer before falling
to the ground.

All that was left of the intelligent creature was a slumped heap of
rusty orange and red.

Jess Goodacre (14)
Ripon Grammar School

The Boy

You caught my eye
you made me tingle
I really hoped that you were single

you were single
now what to do?
I really want to get close to you

get close to you
that's what I thought
these feelings I should have fought

I should have fought
but how?
Now I'm really, really caught

I'm really caught
what should I do?
I think I've fallen in love with you

in love with you
what should I do?
It could never be just us two

just us two
that would be great
but you think of me
as just your mate!

Nikki Stubbs (13)
Ripon Grammar School

Gone!

She's gone
Black, empty words
Nothing to hope for
Never to return.

Just gone
Left a space behind
To be filled but
Nothing can do that.

Nothing can fill
The void
That she left
Nothing can compare.

Rachel Fisken (14)
Ripon Grammar School

Untitled

I know what it's like to be like you;
The sadness and the pain.

I know what it's like to feel like you;
The guilt and the blame.

I know what it's like to see like you;
No future, no plans;

I know what it's like being like you,

But do you know what it's like being me?

Hannah Slater (13)
Ripon Grammar School

TORNADO

The sky was grey and white
The clouds which were cotton
Were now a big blanket
Of swirling smoke. The
Wind suddenly picked up.
The trees rattled their
Leaves. A loud siren
Alarmed me that a
Monstrous tornado
Was approaching!
I hurried to my shelter.
I locked the wood
Doors. I waited
Patiently as
Mother Nature's
Worst nightmare
Passed over my
Weak old home.
The doors rattled. I
Could hear my house
Being wrecked to
Pieces. I stared out,
It was a ghost
Town from an
Unrealistic movie
And
I
Was
There.

Kate McCulloch (14)
Ripon Grammar School

Witches

Dancing around the smoking pot,
Until the stew was nice and hot.
Over this their fitted nails,
They add to this the slimy snails.

Strapping victims to the chair,
Life for them is just unfair,
On their faces a look of fear,
In their eyes rolls a tear.

How they wish for their release,
And that the witches would make peace,
Here the evil witches shout
The sands of time are running out.

Sarah Jawad (14)
Ripon Grammar School

Love

Can you feel it?
Can you describe it?
Is it in the air around us?
Is it marriage, but then there's divorce.
Is it a little schoolgirl crush?
Is it at first sight, when your heart skips a beat?
Is it your job, your home, your family?
Can you fall into it?
Can you fall out of it?
Is it sent from the stars above?
Is it real or is it a dream?
Who can define it?
No one, it seems.

Anna Greenwood (14)
Ripon Grammar School

STARS

Stars shine in the sky
But will they always glisten
'Till the end of time.

Kerrie Gray (14)
Ripon Grammar School

I CAN'T DO POEMS!

I'm not very good at poems
They never look like a poem should
And I can't spell
And even if I wrote a poem, it would
Never be any good.

I just can't work it out!
How do you make it rhyme?
I start with good intentions,
But it ends up a mess every time.

Sarah Walburn (14)
Ripon Grammar School

THE TIGER

He lies patiently
Sifting through the grass meadows
He sinks, he pounces!

Frank Flavell (14)
Ripon Grammar School

Untitled

It has begun, the chase, the ordeal, the uprooting, the
act of violence - as I knew it would.
I was unprepared, uncoordinated, unready, uncertain
and yet it was up to me, I was on my own.
To hide myself or to reveal, only seconds to decide.
They were coming for me, there were more than one,
I was alone, outnumbered, what were my choices?
Yet I should have known I did not belong here.
Not now, I am of the night, the hunter
Now becoming the hunted.
Wherever I hide, it will only be a matter of time.
My fate is decided, there can be no alternative
My language will not be deciphered or understood,
the colour of my skin, or my pleading for
mercy will go unnoticed, unheeded,
I hold my breath for what seems like an eternity
as footsteps approach.
Voices, once friendly, well known are now
menacing, vindictive, intent on capture and humiliation.
It is done, they have me - there is no escape.
It is senseless to struggle, to complain,
to argue my case
I am thrown into the night -
After all - I am just a cat.

Caroline Foster (14)
Ripon Grammar School

Fireworks

Exploding colour
Like a cobweb in the sky
Then darkness again.

Leanne Haswell (14)
Ripon Grammar School

The Other Half

The dress with the stain from a reminiscent night out
and which stain is unknown because of the influence
the influence being just for relaxation and instead turned wild
wild being chained to a lamp post and left till morning
the lamp post where we first met and our kiss that didn't end
a kiss that sealed our pact to be together and resembled as a ring
the ring that was placed on the finger and hand that was shown on the
picture and the picture that showed the scene and the smiles
the smile that continued and grew old together and carried on the pact
a pact that lasted for all eternity
eternity being forever now one half was gone.

Christine Flintoft (15)
Ripon Grammar School

The Sun

Burning ball up in the sky
Giving life to all
Miles away from you and I
It will never fall.

Heat rays beating down on me
From the sky above.
It is there for all to see
Like a thousand doves.

We only see it in the day
Bright, bold and strong.
In the night it hides away
In its course, it moves along.

Jasmine Hatherly (14)
Ripon Grammar School

Classroom Tales

Okay, yeah . . .
Hello!
It's Christmas Eve
I thought about it
That sounds pretty good . . .
Hi!
No!
Shut up!
Creates something . . .
Which one smells?
You could also write this . . .
He's writing!
You can talk about literally anything.
Kind of food . . .
Apricots
You have half a poem to do.
Everybody loves . . .
Your mum goes 'Don't eat them!'
Why the blue?
Right . . .
Sex . . .
Chips . . .
Rock and roll . . .
Two bullets . . .
What else can I do?
What did you say?
Silence!

Chris Legg (15)
Ripon Grammar School

A Long Song

I hate you and all that you stand for
Every day I struggle to appease you.

I fight with you as soon as I awake
Your irrational existence sickens me.

I despise your hypocritical ways
And your stereotypical appearance.

Why do you torture me day and night
In an endless decaying of my soul?

You've shattered my reality
With alarming realism.

It's driving me to the edge
Every time I reluctantly indulge in your presence

Nightmares seem like a refuge
Compared with your ice-cold glove.

Deep inside is a hatred
A dark longing beckons;

The love of pain seems incomprehensible
Yet such pleasures would be welcome.

You are the prison walls that hold me in
You restrict me and I hate you for it.

Just let me be
I want to exist my own way.

Now my soul descends into the crowd,
I am just an epitome of this rationalised society.

I am a concoction of emotions in a canvas shell
That putrefy, and noxiate my essence.

The liberation of my sanity
Is achieved by my endless battle.

I look away from the mirror
And I live for another day.

Craig Swan (14)
Ripon Grammar School

THOUGHTS

Through silence we wait for noise
Through noise we wait for silence
Hypocritical humans stand together in their decisions.
But, for knowing this, am I different, do I stand out?
What makes me realise this, when ignorance was the word,
And still is the word . . . probably always will be the word.
Knowing this is criminal but to lie is right
If it is wrong to lie, how can knowing be criminal?
Is knowing a dark secret hidden away from the world?
And if, if it is
How did I reach it, claim it for my own?
Why is this me, all alone in my thoughts?
Agreeing would be wrong, yet I feel worse in solidarity.
Can good come from this that seems evil?
Will the world one day agree with me?
Then it will be me in unity, me with power
But, but then
Who will have my position? Who will be all alone
In their thoughts, destroying their mind trying to answer?
Will my joy always cause others pain?
Is it meant to be like this? Questioning
Your every move. Always wondering.

Sarah Mason (15)
Ripon Grammar School

My Prejudiced Views

My own conscience smashed by perfection's, specifications,
Lies of socialisation, rationalised stereotypes
You can crush me but not my views
Lies
Your views are not your own but those of
This hypocritical legion - named society.
Truth
True
Believe their lies but your lies may not
be believed
That which is innocent proven guilty
Impure virgin

David Hirst (14)
Ripon Grammar School

Dreams

I am here
Now I'm not,
All these things I'll forget
All these people I have met.

Am I in the dream or
Is the dream in me?

I was there
Now I'm not,
All these things I'll forget
All these people I had met.

I am the dream or
Is the dream me?

Jeremy Wright (14)
Ripon Grammar School

TIME

Past, present, future
All are in the past

Past, the forgotten time
Moved memories of the mind
Dreams and reality many of good
Are lost in the subconscious mind
Others of evil, grind away
Until the end of time
Never forgotten but never remembered.

Present, the time of now
The time of what if?
Stopping every second
But always moving
The time of colour.

Future, the time to come
The time of grey
The unpredictable time
The time of darkness.

Jonathan Stirling (14)
Ripon Grammar School

NIGHTMARES

Alone in the dark;
Only my nightmares and me.
Please, please wake me up!

Shaun Wilson (14)
Ripon Grammar School

The Scapegoat

They cursed me,
called me names
and swore at me too,
they took me to the desert
and I stopped . . .

. . . Dead

I walked and walked,
ran and ran
through highs and lows.
Storms and river flows
every image a vivid picture . . .
. . . That wasn't really there.

All I could feel was the heat
and the hot sand beneath my hoof.
Plodding along with my life flowing out
I wanted to shout
but I was there alone . . .
. . . Nobody around to hear my sound.

I am left
dying with life flowing out.
I want to know why,
why was it me?
All I can see is the sand . . .
. . . Just the sand, sand, sand, sand sand

Tim Casson (14)
Ripon Grammar School

The Swan

The mist rolled in around the lake
The owls came in to roost.
The swans sleek body swept around the moonlit bend
But
Something was wrong . . .

The swan's elegant neck was hanging low
As though its heart was breaking.

Trailing through the sagging reeds
A silver flash of fishing tackle.

The swan lifted up its head
And the most beautiful voice was sounded.

A cross between angel's singing
And the wind blowing through, blowing through the reeds.

For three hours the sound went on
Sometimes high, sometimes low
But never breaking
But
With only seconds to live
The sound caught in its throat,
And a shining white light
Appeared like a halo around the swan,
And it disappeared from this Earth.
Into another time and space far, far from here.

Katherine Clements (14)
Ripon Grammar School

CRUSH

Counting every second
Wanting every hour.
Imagining the meeting
and the force that it would create.
Feeling each touch,
even though it hasn't happened.
My being isn't good enough for him,
but all my wishes focus on its change.
Why am I me? Am I me?
Or is this someone's dream.
In my dream we combine,
In his I don't exist.
What attracts my subconscious to another?
Why is it so strongly done?
I still imagine the power,
but the deed will remain on the shelf,
covered in dust.

Sarah Green (15)
Ripon Grammar School

SAQLAIN MUSHTAQ

When you want it
You can't have it

When you get it
You don't want it

It's the desire
Not the possession.

Jimmy Martin (15)
Ripon Grammar School

DARK

While the stars shine
like candles in a darkened room.
The curtains close and lights are put out.
One by one, the fires die down
and peace washes through the valleys.
Dreams are caught in the frosty air
and float like clouds into the sky.
And while the stars shine
the world is at rest.

Nothing dares move through the silence
as the population lies down to rest.
No animal stirs as he passes
through the land.
His darkness is eerie
and his power is vast.

The moon gently glides across the sky,
illuminating the darkened land.
Silently he passes, silently he leaves.
The sun like a blazing ball of fire
appears on the horizon. Casting
light across the land. As it rises
into the sky.

He's gone.

Michelle Harvey (15)
Ripon Grammar School

SHIPWRECKED

In good weather and a calm sea,
It moved as smoothly as a well-oiled machine;
Familiar sounds and creaks,
To the people on board anyway;
It had a mass of tangled ropes and rigging,
With bulging sails too.

But it was rough weather,
And the sea was stormy.
Well, stormy off the Cornish coast;
Vicious jagged rocks approached now.

A scrape, a bump,
Nothing much.
The hold took on an extra load,
A cargo of water;
Boats were lowered, men jumped overboard,
As the ship disappeared from view for the final time.

Tom Franklin (15)
Ripon Grammar School

THE TRAMP

A dark day dawning
The clouds rush by
The wind whistles through the trees
Sending leaves spiralling upwards

Caterpillars of cars weaving their way
School children stamping through puddles
In a doorway sits someone
Blanket wrapped and homeless.

Laura Illingworth (15)
Ripon Grammar School

The Way I Wanna Die

I'm falling deeper
there is no turning back
and I know the pain is going to become sweeter

I'm falling deeper
running towards the light
I can smell it as the pleasure comes to a peak

I'm stuck here now
seeing the sounds
and all while I wish I never was

The pain is coming now
no more pleasure
I think I'm starting to hear the colours

I'm coming up now
back from the murky depths
I dream of a shining saviour following me

I can feel the light now
burning my skin
I start to sweat while my surface starts to shiver

I am warm now
safety and security surrounds me
I am being taken away to be healed and helped

but in vain

Russell Gibson (15)
Ripon Grammar School

My Dream

It was a strange dream
That made me think a lot
Now my mind is made up.
I must tell my friend.
Though she will not like it,
It was very special to me.

I spent it with a gentleman
Who gave me a special time.
He owns an expensive car
In which we first made love.
My friend will be jealous
As he is who she loves.

I know I cannot tell her
That I have found my only love
Because he is her lover
Who doesn't love my friend.
I've told him to tell her
But he always tells me 'No!'

I can make him happy
And that he sure does know.
But how can he hurt her
As she loves him so.
But as he wouldn't let you go
I could see only one way out.

Helen Darbyshire (15)
Ripon Grammar School

Oblivion

All eyes look towards the heavens
Voices sound as one in joy and hope
Then
Thoughts become entwined with
visions of death and fire.
The mist surrounds all -
an encompassing blanket of darkness.
The stars rip through the blackness
and look in horror upon the scene
that awaits them.

Don't look down!

Screams ring out through the tortured silence,
The sun shines cold upon the desolate landscape.
The fallen angels weep
with tears
of despair.
The deed is done.

Don't look down!
Or you might fall
Into the
abyss.

Victoria Gardner (15)
Ripon Grammar School

Fit For A King

Comfort could not compete with the pleasure he desired
so greed made the decision.
But even the pleasure persuaded him to choose
between honesty and further pursuit.
Careless that to acquire such
greed grew into murder
resulting in murder pursuing greed
becoming a vicious circle.

Natalie Henderson (15)
Ripon Grammar School

Skool Skate Relief

The day is long, a drag.
Yet at night it all begins.
The flow, the air, the wind
The noise, a constant rumble
That relaxes you and identifies you.

The night is long yet it flows
It's your inspiration, it's you.
The crack of a whip
The constant bombardment of clatters.
That relaxes you and identifies you.

Christopher Kane (15)
Ripon Grammar School

Maniacs

People are so cruel
They don't care what harm they cause
It makes me hate life.

Heidi Fraser (15)
Ripon Grammar School

Hopes And Fears

My hopes and fears.
My hopes.
My fears.
I fear drugs.
I hope for peace.
I fear poverty.
I hope for a happy family.
I fear death.
I hope for birth.
I fear guns.
I hope for friends.
I fear pain.
I hope for fun times.
I fear the world ending.
But when I'm born
These fears become real
And the dreams become my
Hopes.

Thomas Johann (13)
Rossett School

LETTING GO OF MY LIFE

My name is Rebecca Wood
Becky to you.
I died on July 28th
My horse Meg fell on me.
It was a tragic experience
As I felt my life slip away . . .

My mother said I could go to horse camp.
They asked me my name and age.
'Becky, I said. '14' I said.
I got a beautiful grey mare, Meg.
I was over the moon.
We did cantering, trotting and galloping
But one thing I had been so excited about,
Jumping.

I loved watching it on TV.
The day came, I was last in line.
At last my time came,
I cantered up to it and jumped.
Something went wrong, Meg bucked
I went flying over the fence and Meg
followed and landed on top of me.
She tried to get up but landed back on top of me.
I slowly slipped away.
I slowly let go of my life.

Kerry-Anne Durrant (13)
Rossett School

The Groat

I was weeding one summer's afternoon
And I found a thin piece of copper;
At first I thought that it was a rock,
So I left it on the kitchen table.

My daughter took it to school
And there she found out it was a 'groat'.
She came running home fast
She was panting very hard, hard as a train
She muttered 'It was a groat!'

Many people at school act like
I was in for the money.
I get upset when they do
But I didn't really care.
All that interests me and my dad
Is the age of the coin.

It is aged from 1279 to 1500
Maybe more.
My teacher said
It was from Edward III's reign.
Which I thought was good, in fact
Fantastic!

Christine Wilson (13)
Rossett School

Deserted Desert

The deserted desert lies
beneath the burning sun.
Soundless and hot,
Never-ending, far into the horizon.
The spiny cactus stands
in the sun's rays.

Creeping reptiles creep through
dry sands.
A cool breeze flows through
spiky cacti,
But still, soundless and hot.

The sun dies down, down
and down,
Till day turns to night.

    Dark,
    Deserted
    and
    Dead!

Sonia Riyat (11)
Rossett School

Salad Cream

Salad cream is going away
It's going, going, gone.
It's been a dressing for many years
And now it's been taken away.

The sales have dropped
Shoppers have stopped
Buying wonderful salad cream.

Mayonnaise is going strong
But the fact is I will still long
For my salad cream.

My sandwich won't taste the same
The bread will be dry.
I wish the salad cream sales
Were not going down the drain.

Robert Grimwood (13)
Rossett School

Deserted Island

The beautiful golden sand,
The clear deep blue ocean.
All is not stirred,
On this sandy deserted island.

All of a sudden a gush of wind
blows over the sands,
And the ocean ripples.
A mighty rage of thunder hits and a flash
Of lightning strikes the treetops.

The storm destroys the palm trees,
The wind swirls the sand into the air.
The birds all squawk and all nature
Is disturbed.

The wind starts to drop,
The sea calms.
And all is left destroyed,
The island aches and quietly bleeds.

Gemma Blades (11)
Rossett School

TRAIN CRASH

The train was coming down the line,
People on the way to work,
Some people kissed their families goodbye for the day,
They didn't know it would be over.

The train was coming down the line
At about five to eight,
In that split second at 8 o'clock both trains collided,
The carriages burst into flames.

The train was coming down the line,
This couldn't be prevented,
That tragic day won't go away
For many years to come.

The train was coming . . .

Iain Walker (14)
Rossett School

HALLOWE'EN

Each year on Hallowe'en night!
Something comes to your door to give you a fright.
Inside your home you're as safe as can be
But what lies outside that you can't see?
Although you don't know it, all around the streets,
Are ghosts and ghouls who you don't want to meet!
Wandering around are witches too,
And vampires holding pumpkins which stare at you!
When they reach your door, they call 'trick or treat',
But you don't answer, all you can hear is your heartbeat!
Inside you know, it's all just a game,
But it scares you to death, and it's all such a shame!

Hayley Wood (13)
Rossett School

My Little Brother

He bounds in from outside
Disturbing the peace in an instant.
He yells 'You'll never guess what I did today!'
(Sometimes I wonder where the mute button is).

He's really sweet sometimes
When he's snug asleep in bed.
Or when he's on his best, best behaviour
Because there's something he wants.

But most of the time he's just plain fun,
And good to have around.
He does his silly dance or his funny faces
That never fails
To bring a smile,
That's my bother *Jack!*

Amy Fawdington (11)
Rossett School

Autumn

Yellow, brown and red leaves fall from the trees.
Trees we see bare, way up high.
Hazel brown conkers fall and split on the ground
The wild, wild wind whistles through the trees
And makes us all glad to be indoors.
The dew makes our feet wet as we trudge to school.
Wet soggy leaves stuck to the floor,
Grandad sweeps them up once more.

Natalie Ward (11)
Rossett School

WINTER GARDEN

Wintertime is here
Birds fly south 'til next year.
The robins peck and fight
Over a piece of food in sight.

The snow is falling to the ground,
Making a peaceful sound.
It covers streets and gardens
And makes them look so neat.

The garden is covered in white
Not a speck of grass in sight.
As winter is here,
Birds fly south 'til next year.

The winter garden's snowy white
Gleams on me.
As white rose bushes pop out to see
A little hedgehog scares a bee.

The snow falls to the ground
Now there is no sound.
As snowball fights go on
You know winter has come!

Adrian Wintersgill (11)
Rossett School

THE BEACH

The beach is misty and foggy,
It should be sunny and sandy,
But people use it as a litter bin.
Day in, day out, litter piles up on it.
Pollution chokes the animals that live there.
What did they do?

The beach is giving up hope of ever being pure again.
It's giving up on its once long ago human friends.
Day in, day out it tries to wash its waves on the shore,
But pollution chokes it.
What did it do?

Melanie Speight (12)
Rossett School

FUTURE DREAMS

Dear baby Katalin,

You're 11 months
old, so small in this large world. So innocent yet so
naive in this rather cruel world. Sometimes I watch you lie
there, sound asleep wondering what you will grow up to
become. Hoping never to be involved in drugs, praying you'll never
experience poverty like the children I have seen in Turkey. I remember
a little boy about 10 years old carrying his 4 year old sister on his
back, making a living polishing shoes, their only way of survival, then
no home to return to, just a shop doorway! And children who are half
beaten to death by their alcoholic mothers and fathers. Hundreds of
children suffer abuse every day. Also the many diseases that touch lives
every day. Just as you came into this world my auntie left,
dying from cancer.
The wars, fighting and brutal killings of today, many people are
affected each day.
But my hopes for you are that you shall lead a happy life
and make each day count.

Jenny Marks (13)
Rossett School

What The Future Holds For You

I fear for World War III and much more poverty,
I hope for world peace and less people on the street,
More cash in my pocket but drugs can hop it,
Good health should be free and less use for weaponry,
Technology will improve and bad people will be on the move,
For you I leave this future,
So good it may look to be,
For you I leave this future,
Stay drug free,
For you I leave this future,
Make good use of it, for me.

Simon Green (13)
Rossett School

Stormy Sea

The sea crashes
against the helpless rocks.
Foam rises into the rainy air
and the swollen waves
drive on.
The sea once blue
now a stormy grey.
Like a dark cloud
full of anger
and swallowing anyone in sight.
Waves hit each other
and become more confident
and this time attack all the rocks.

Adam Farrell (11)
Rossett School

Peace Has Come

The guns have stopped.
The killing has stopped.
The dying has stopped.
The birds are singing.
The children are playing.
Fields are full of crops and cattle.
Clean water from the town pump.
Poverty, famine gone.
Death has gone.
There is glory, prizes and praise
To those who brought peace.
Those who brought war are dead.
The war is over.

Chris Beecroft (14)
Rossett School

Cornflake!

He's gigantic, as big as a cat,
White like a snowball,
He loves running in the garden,
Eating all my mum's plants . . .
She's so happy about this!
Dandelions are his favourite food.
His pink eyes stare at you,
His ears jump up at a sound of a pin dropping,
He is my Cornflake,
The *best bunny on Earth!*

Alice Jackson (11)
Rossett School

The Wild Horse

The wild horse gallops in the dark,
Through the mist and fog,
His rider urging him on,
When they come to a sudden halt
As a rabbit gives the horse the spooks,
Even faster he carries on,
A girl watches the black horse and his
rider from her window.
They danced with the wind,
They looked free like the wind,
Free and happy, alive and wild,
But as quickly as they came,
They were gone,
Gone, but not forgotten!

Lauren Jay Carrington (11)
Rossett School

The Haunted House

Screaming in the dungeons
And howling in the hall,
All the ghouls and ghosts come out
When the moon is full.

Growling in the cupboards
And movement in the library,
Hear the chime of the grandfather clock
As it strikes twelve ominously.

Laughing in the cellar
And creaking in the loft,
Watch the shadows in front of you
As they dart across the room.

Screeching in the ballroom
And groaning in the study,
When you think you're scared enough
Run right out the door!

Mark Simpson (12)
Rossett School

My Son

My hopes for you son are very clear,
I hope that your life will bring all that you hold dear,
My parents had their own expectations of me,
I thought that they were being over protective you see,
When they reeled off a list of all that they wished for from me.
But after having a child, my own flesh and blood,
Each day I count my blessings and thank the Lord above,
For giving me something more precious than money can buy,
And I pray that one day you'll understand why,
I've written to you in the way that I have.
Sometimes I will shout and make you feel sad,
You may even say, 'I hate you, Dad,'
I know those words aren't really true,
Remember son, I was a child too.
And no matter where I am, abroad or at home,
You'll always be with me son, you'll never be alone.

Paul Dixon (13)
Rossett School

SWAN TROUBLE!

It happened a long time ago,
I think, when I was three,
We were feeding the greedy ducks
And Mum gave some bread to me.

We were going to have a photo,
I was standing unaware
Of the huge great white swan
Standing right behind me there.

The bread was in my hand,
The swan nicked it for a meal,
It snatched at it and ran away,
Did you know that swans could steal?

I decided to chase after it
For I was really cross,
I ran my very fastest
To show that I was boss.

The swan went in the water
For I was much too slow,
I had only just recovered
In time for the photo.

When we left the park
I was really glad,
The swan swam serenely on
It could not make me sad.

Jade Wellington Graham (11)
Rossett School

Future Hopes

Dear baby Jake,

You're so small and too helpless in this world
to see what the world is really like.
There is war just around the corner,
Drugs down the street,
Poverty and violence,
Racism and diseases.
Hopefully you won't need to see this.
Hopefully there will be an end to this before you're my age.
Hopefully you won't need to go through an earthquake,
poverty, racism or pollution.
There is a lot of money on this Earth but yet there is still a
Third World debt.
People are really selfish and don't seem to care.
People die and babies are born every second.
Hopefully you will make a
difference in this millennium.
Hopefully there will be an end
to stealing, violence and people
carelessly polluting this Earth.
I will always love you and I want you to know
I will protect you and take care
of you.
I don't want you to see children
being beaten, people having no homes
to go to.
Innocent people being killed in wars,
Children looking after brothers and sisters
because their mum or dad are too drunk to care.

Natalie Jamieson (13)
Rossett School

The Things In Life

The long winter days as I stand on my own,
No one to talk to, no one at all.
There's people that come
And people who go,
Not saying a lot,
Not talking at all.

They came up to me
And started to talk,
Now they're my friends
We play and we whisper
Our secrets are ours.

The guns and the fighting,
The wars and the killing,
The terrible things
The world has to bring.

Peace, peace, glorious peace,
No guns, no killing,
Just the sun coming up
And the sun going down.

Alison Hart (13)
Rossett School

Ghosts

Slowly he awakens
From his shabby grave.
He looks around expectantly,
Wondering,
'Did I die for a reason?
Why was it a lonely death?'
Mortified at what he sees:

People homeless on the streets,
Children taken from their mother's side,
Murders happening across the world,
People bullied out of their wits,
Burglars taking an advantage . . .
He returns to rest
In *anger!*

Beth Crawley (11)
Rossett School

WAR!

As the night grew dark,
The wind grew rough,
And the rain came pouring down,
The soldiers just waited silently,
Smoking, smoking as many cigarettes as they can,
Then . . .
Boom!
A shell hit.

The soldiers ran out of the trenches
Charging at the enemy.
All you hear is *slash, bang, slash, bang,*
Then silence . . .
Bombers flew over and dropped their load.
Three hours after . . .
Medics come pouring in,
Bodies everywhere.

When they got home . . .
They are sleeping,
Sleeping in . . .
Coffins.

Ashley Rodney (11)
Rossett School

The Ballad Of Alan Heywood

Alan Heywood was a climber,
He got his fun, from climbing high.
Ever fearless, an old timer,
Never thinking, that he would die.

Alan, he was from Accrington,
Accrington is in Lancashire.
He liked to be, out in the sun,
His climbing skills, would never tire.

At the age of just forty-one,
He climbed the rocks, up to the sky.
He'd climbed them all, he'd had some fun,
He didn't realise he would die.

He was an expert climber then,
He worked with five mates, as a team.
There was a crowd watching of ten,
As he fell, someone gave a scream.

He was soon rescued from Mont Blanc,
They slid him onto a stretcher.
They took him away in a tank,
And stood beside was a sketcher.

He soon went into a coma,
This was a shame, for his family.
They all left him and, said 'Loner,'
He looked just like a squashed brambly.

His family turned off the life-support,
They didn't stay, to say goodbye.
There was a newspaper report,
The family said, it told a lie.

Marie Dalby (12)
Rossett School

PARENT PAMPER PINCHER

In Holland where the tulips grow,
There was a man called Edward Crow,
With hair of black and eyes of blue,
He stood tall, nearly six foot two.

It was a windy day that day,
All the tree's leaves had blown away.
When Ed and his son, Roger went
To the Magical Kiddies tent.

In this gigantic kiddies store,
There were toys, food and lots, lots more.
The gifts were stacked from wall to wall,
Toys for all ages, big and small.

But Ed and Roger passed all that,
To buy other things free of VAT.
To the nappy section they went,
Rushing through the magical tent.

Ed looks around, picks up Pampers,
Slides them in his shopping hamper.
To the main exit he does go,
On the camera this does show!

'Stop thief!' shouts the angry shopkeeper,
Now Ed knows he must be fleeter.
A sweat had formed on his forehead,
Then the assistant shouts, 'It's Ed!'

Ed turns and runs out of the shop,
Leaving the hamper with the cop,
In the panic he also left
Rog to take the blame for the theft!

Sarah Birse (12)
Rossett School

A Mystery Sub

A mystery sub was seen
By a man nicknamed Mr Sheen.
He alerted his generals
Who called out the federals.

The search was captained by a man
Who used to work on a large dam.
They did look high and they looked low
But the submarine would not show.

They searched around the Swedish coast,
One of the searchers saw a ghost.
They said it was the sub's first mate
Who clearly met a nasty fate.

They did call the US navy,
Some even got drunk on gravy.
The navy took over the 'gaff'
And all that they found was really 'naff'.

Off the Swedish coast it happened,
Some just wish it never happened
Because it's all over the news,
Some are having the bad search blues.

They publicly admitted
They really should have quitted
To save the public earache
From choppers keeping them awake.

It took six weeks to sort this out
But the navy went out with a shout,
Hip, hip, hooray they all shouted
And nobody even bouted.

Ben Fox (12)
Rossett School

Bridal Ballad

All the good friends of John Hacketts
Wore beautiful blue silk jackets.
John wore a top hat and silk tails,
While his best man kept him on the rails.

The wedding was held in Hampshire,
It was all that they could desire.
And was held on the 7th of May
On a bright and breezy spring day.

When Jason King got really, really drunk,
He called the best man a smelly skunk.
It started a really big fight
Which lasted right into the night.

As the police squad attended
Jason was soon apprehended.
And the policewoman did squeal
As Tracy hit her with her heel.

Soon all the guests were arrested
And all were swiftly breath tested.
Tracy was put in a dirty cell
And Jason was locked up as well.

Some were made to pay a large fine,
While others were not allowed wine.
Which shows they all had little brains
To cause other people such pain.

John and his wife had a good life
Without too much trouble and strife.
They lived to be very old
And had six children, so we're told.

Adam Ketteringham (12)
Rossett School

The Man And The Baby

Walking round in a store
One bright and sunny day,
A man in the country of Holland
Smelled something and walked away.

He didn't know what it was
Until the baby he was with
Started to giggle quite loudly
At the way the man did sniff.

The man turned the corner
And looked around.
The aisle was bare,
It was nappies he'd found!

He made up his mind
And started to snatch.
For his breath
He needed to catch.

Then an officer
Passed on by,
Seeing the man
And thinking, 'Oh my!'

The man had heard
And looked around.
He saw the officer,
Nappies were on the ground.

The man ran off
So full of shame,
Leaving the baby
To take the blame.

Jennifer Crowl (12)
Rossett School

The Gunman

The gunman gets into his car,
He drives whilst eating a cream bun,
He drives past an old broken bar,
He leaves the old car with his gun.

He walks up to the big black gate,
He opens it with a loud creak,
He climbs the steps at a quick rate,
When he stops his boots make a squeak.

He pointed the gun at the door,
He loaded and took careful aim,
He shot straight in the big, poor door,
It began to thunder and rain.

The family cowered inside,
They barred the door with the settee,
They decided where they would hide,
It was an awful sight to see.

The shots they echoed through the air,
A worried neighbour looked outside,
She ran to the phone in despair,
Called the police and spoke to Sergeant Ryde.

Sergeant Ryde claps on the handcuffs
And pushes the gunman in the car.
The ride to the station was rough,
The journey was ever so far.

Six months later he goes to court,
He's found guilty of the crime.
Five years in jail the jury thought
Would help him change his ways in time.

Philip Cushley (12)
Rossett School

One Saturday Morning

It was a Saturday morning
And in the foggy, scary mist
The couple went in the dawning
And under the sun they kissed.

They put on their car rally kits,
They were black and white and yellow.
What was lying in the pits?
The poor old silly fellows.

They got over to the races
In their TVR two-seater car.
They set themselves their own pace,
Their wheels screeching on the tar.

They were roaring down the track
In car number sixty-five,
And in her stomach the precious pack,
So very glad to be alive.

Then their wheels skidded on the ground,
They knew their end was coming.
Their life was then suddenly torn
As their car just kept on tumbling.

'Carry me home' cried Mother.
'We lie here in a very big pit
And our son won't have a brother.
My poor mother will have a fit.'

But now you're dead
And I will now pray every day
For the one thing that I did love
Has now just flown away.

Charlotte Cottrell (12)
Rossett School

In The Boot For 70 Miles

It was a calm Wednesday morning,
The sun was beaming from the clouds,
England was at its dawning,
And the birds were singing out loud.

That very nice policeman, Bill
Was on his three hour shift that day.
Driving around, ready to kill,
It was only the middle of May!

He saw two men changing a wheel
Or even removing it well.
Luckily he'd had a nice meal
So energy he had to tell.

He confronted them to ask why
But did they listen, did they tell?
He asked us why, oh my,
Not aloud, does that ring a bell?

He got thrown into a big boot
And driven 70 miles.
The car stopped and he heard a 'toot',
His head was in swirly spirals.

Suddenly the boot opened wide,
His mouth dropped open, to his surprise.
He was free so he jumped outside
And undid all the rope and ties.

He went straight to hospital
To seek medical attention.
He had sprained his ankle, that's all,
Any questions you want answered?

Anna Thompson (12)
Rossett School

THE NAPPY NICKER

A man and his son from Holland,
Enjoying a bit of shopping,
Buying some food that is canned,
And a massive ball of white string.

I don't think they can afford much,
I will tell you why I think that,
Stealing nappies, just with a touch,
Hiding them where the baby's sat.

What are they? Are they Dutch Pampers?
Are they the most expensive make?
Now behind the tents for campers,
Trying to make the crime look fake.

But look, the man's now panicking,
It looks as if he's going to run.
He lifts up his ball of white string,
Look he runs. Now he's having fun!

He was seen by security,
They ran, trying to catch the guy.
He managed to escape you see,
He was hard to catch, like a fly.

He's a really uncaring dad,
Ran away and left his baby.
I mean he really must be mad,
How's he gonna tell his lady?

They cannot find the baby's mum,
So they put him into care.
But he's now got a childhood chum,
And stealing, this baby won't dare.

Gavin Russell (12)
Rossett School

PC Breaks Siege

One lunchtime a vicious gunman
Was stopped by a policeman,
He was in the middle of a crime
That had been going on for some time.

The single offender was armed
But was not a threat when disarmed.
A pistol and shotgun were seized
And everybody present was relieved.

It brought a sudden conclusion
With a degree of confusion
To an incident six hours long,
They all felt like singing a song.

In total, held there were seven,
They thought they would end up in heaven.
Four men, two kids and their mum,
Not one of them thought it was fun.

The gunman was twenty-three years old,
He was calculating and cold.
When questioned on the use of force
He was quiet and showed no remorse.

He's appearing at the local court,
His plea shouldn't take much thought,
All the evidence will soon prove
That he definitely made the wrong move.

If they reach a guilty verdict
It will be easy to predict
That he, I'm sure without fail
Will spend a long, long time in jail.

Matthew Day (12)
Rossett School

Peter The Nappy Nicker

It was not a very nice day,
It was right at the end of May,
In the region of Amsterdam,
Peter had just stepped off a tram.

He walked along by the water
Whilst carrying his young daughter,
She started to bawl, squeal and scream!
And he thought, 'Is this a bad dream?'

His daughter, whose name was Ellie
Had done something rather smelly!
Poor Peter was right out of cash,
Into the shop he made a dash.

He ran to the nearest nappy
To try and make Ellie happy,
He tucked it under his jacket
Along with another packet!

As he ran across to the door
Little Ellie fell to the floor.
He panicked and then left her there,
He ran through the door in despair!

He had just ran out of the shop
When he bumped right into a cop!
He pushed past him and got away,
Poor Ellie was left there all day!

Since then Peter was never caught,
And poor Ellie was nearly bought!
Peter rescued her just in time,
And I hope this poem did rhyme!

Laura Town (12)
Rossett School

Policeman Driven 70 Miles In Boot

Sergeant Sturgeon, aged twenty-nine
Has been a policeman a long time.
But in his time in Clackmanshire
Not many crimes have involved tyres!

Today when he stopped, for his lunch
He left his car to have a munch.
Upon his return, from his meal
He saw two men remove a wheel.

He gave a shout and both the men
Ran at him with the strength of ten.
Poor Bill was stuffed into a boot
With the tyre and assorted loot!

The car set off despite Bill's threat,
The driver red and full of sweat.
Along the road towards Carlisle,
Bill kicking hard for miles and miles.

Seventy miles, then out of fuel,
Recriminations - what a fool!
Both men got out and ran away,
'Leave the copper,' Bill heard them say.

A passer-by ended Bill's plight
With good ears and excellent sight!
He saw the boot move up and down,
And prised it open with a frown.

Sergeant Bill radioed to base
To get some help to make the chase.
With both men caught he now must go . . .
On the A74 to Glasgow!

Andrew Kenyon (12)
Rossett School

My Ballad

Sergeant Bill Sturgeon, twenty-nine,
Was walking along, feeling fine,
Back to his car where it had been
Left there for two minutes or three.

When Bill got back to the lay-by
He let out a worried cry
Because he got a big surprise,
So bad he thought that he might die.

There were two men knelt on the ground,
And then when they looked up they found
Sergeant Bill Sturgeon watching them
Nicking his wheels, watching the men.

One was short and fat and podgy,
He looked like he was quite dodgy.
The other was tall and skinny
With ears so big he looked like Minnie.

Bill punched the fat man with his fist,
Then punched the tall man and got kicked.
They bashed Bill's head on a sharp rock,
And then Bill passed out from the shock.

When Bill awoke he was quite scared
For where he was he was unaware.
But actually he was in
The boot of a car, filled with gin.

But he pulled himself together,
Took off his jacket made of leather,
Used a crowbar, opened the lid,
Informed his colleagues, that was it.

Alice Gostling (12)
Rossett School

Shoplifting Nappies

It was on a Monday morning
Dad woke up to the smell of poo.
He staggered about yawning
No nappies in - what should he do?

Father and son dashed off to the shops,
For their emergency dash.
Halfway there his heart went drop,
He'd set off without any cash.

He had no time to go back home,
So he kept going straight on.
There was no time to go to a phone,
And the first shop he went to had none.

An idea came into his head,
He picked up some nappies and ran.
If he got caught he'd surely be dead,
How he wished he now had a van.

He turned and ran for his life,
With nappies under his arm.
How would he explain to his wife,
That he had really meant no harm.

He kept on running as fast as he could,
What a stupid thing he had done.
As he approached a nearby wood,
He realised he'd forgotten his son!

The sirens were going off loudly,
The poor baby was still crying.
The policeman caught him proudly,
Because he'd stolen instead of buying.

Paul Margis (12)
Rossett School

WHEN A DAY AT THE RACES IS RUINED

My Mary Jane, you had a boy
And now you are to have one other
To each I give a single toy
To dear Fredrick and his brother.

I heard your dear old father say
That to the race track you will go
I hope you have a smashing day
I'll listen on the radio.

So off you went to race a car
That hard race track held all your fate
Why did you go off road so far?
So when you saw it was too late.

I see you lie on your deathbed
You look at peace with no worries
A ring of roses round your head
The pain in my heart still buries.

Why did you go off yesterday?
You don't even like the race track
Death was the price you had to pay
For that you will never come back.

I'll look after your other son
Unfortunate as it may be
I'll tell Fredrick you're having fun
Above the clouds and all the sea.

So now I leave you both to rest
To let the angels take you
The years of your life were the best
And the years of your father too.

Elinor Dean (13)
Rossett School

Ballad

Alan Haywood was 41,
and a climber from Accrington.
He slid, fell, and banged his head,
on Mont Blanc, where all thought he was dead.

He lay in a daze in the snow,
waiting because he did not know,
frostbite would quickly set in,
body give up and mind give in.

Rescue came, he was unaware,
he was taken with extra care,
to base camp where a doctor said,
'Hospital - before he's dead!'

Doctors tended him for days
'til stable, to be sent away,
to the hospital near his home,
where his wife could see him alone.

His coma lasted many days,
his wife she saw how still he lay,
in silence on the life-support
no reactions, flickers, she thought.

He climbed Mont Blanc and achieved,
'twas what he'd wished and believed,
to reach the top of this mountain
to be remembered by his name.

Before the switch was turned off,
his wife prayed that he might cough
but now his life has been spent
he died from his back being bent!

Christian Thomas (12)
Rossett School

THE NAPPY NAPPER

Allan Martin was forty-one
He was bold, brave and full of fun.
With hair of black and eyes of blue,
Allan Martin wore smart clothes which were new.

In Holland near by the blue sea,
Allan lives with his family.
Near the town on a quiet street,
Allan's children lay fast asleep.

The sun rises in the morning,
Tired Allan wakes up yawning.
Baby stirs and then starts crying,
End of peace, thinks Allan sighing.

Baby cries and will not settle,
Allan then puts on the kettle.
Baby still seems very restless,
Time to go out to stop the stress.

It was a hot day in the town,
Where everyone seemed to be down.
There was Allan pushing a pram,
He was shopping in Amsterdam.

He went into the babies store,
There were clothes, toys and a lot more.
He picked up some nappies to take,
Walked to the door and made a break.

He was stopped as he ran away
He will never forget that day.
As he fled in fear and worry,
Left the baby in a hurry.

Lindsey Skeels (13)
Rossett School

Lost

Trees creak, owls hoot
Then silence, eerie silence.
Darkness, like a thick black blanket
Hangs all around me.
What's that noise?
Leaves rustle, foxes howl
Then silence, deafening silence.
Footsteps - quiet, scraping, following me.
Heart-thumping, palms sweating,
Where to go?
Start to run, feet pounding like beating
drums
Stop!
Chest heaving, breath gasping
Must keep going.
Branches grabbing, creepers clinging
Dragging me back.
Hand on shoulder
Scream!

Sam Ford (11)
Ryedale School

Loneliness

A dull December's day
With no one to talk to,
The smell of pollution
the smell of ice.
I see the fogginess
I can feel the snow.
I see spider's webs that look like snowflakes,
I'm in the woods with no one around.

Michelle Humphrey (14)
Ryedale School

THE MOORS

The grass blowing against my legs, tingling through me.
Cows as small as toys, chew greenery down below me.
The sky looks happy, and is bright blue high up above me.
A rainbow far away, the colours stream and stretch over me.
Some sheep plod up the track, stumbling gingerly behind me.
The wind, sharp but welcoming, whistles a harmony throughout me.
A river rushing against the rocks, lapping, refreshing in the valley
beneath me.
One taste of clean fresh air, as I inhale it inside me.
Becks and springs gurgle and moss cushions my fall underneath me.
Fields of rocks, heather and rivers waiting to be explored, thought
loses me.
A pretty sunset painted purple, red, pink and yellow glows distant
from me.
Then a black starry darkness, still and silent is listening for me.
Except for the wind cooling me
As I walk down from the windswept moor, bitter cold, my thoughts
warm me.

Hannah Winters (11)
Ryedale School

THE REAL SUN

I know what the sun is really like
Its shape, its colour, its looks.
You think you know, but not with your eyes
You've only read it in books.

Astronomers say it's a yellow colour
Rather like a ball.
But they've not been and they've not seen
They think they know it all.

Opticians say don't look at the sun,
Or it will damage your sight.
So you'll never know what's really up there
Because of that tremendous light.

I love the sun, we are good friends
And I meet with him at noon.
He hangs there in the dazzling light
And promises me the moon.

Muireann Price (12)
Ryedale School

I Wonder!

I wonder
What will the Earth be like in the next millennium?
Will computers teach us?
Will we go to a virtual school?
Will monkeys talk?
What will the world be like?
Will we have cyber-pets and whizz-kid vets?
Will dogs still be alive?
Will we inhabit outer space?
or be taken by another race?
What will cars look like?
Will a kid still ride a bike?
Will we live on Mars or the moon?
I'm so glad it's coming soon!
Will humans exist at all,
or will the sun burn out?
We live to know,
that's what the future
is all about.
I wonder?

Oliver Harrison (13)
Ryedale School

Scared

Inside a gloomy place,
Stone walls painted black,
But the paint is chipping off,
Between the stones light sneaks through.
There are windows with hardly any glass in,
It's all over the floor.
The ceiling is a mucky white,
With cobwebs in the corners.
The floor is rough and grey,
With stones and glass on it.
There is a sound like owls whistling,
But it's very faint and I can just hear it.
There is smoke outside coming in through the
Window.
I can taste it as it puffs in.
I feel *scared!*

Jodie Tateson (11)
Ryedale School

Will The Millennium Be A Paradise?

Sea animals frolicking in the crystal-filled sea.
The sun's golden runway for the snow-white gulls to land.
On the edge of the world tiny boats balance with care.
Specks ruffling up the covers of the giant's bed.

Upside down, white islands drift on the pale blue sea.
The massive ocean all locked into one tiny shell.
Castles, channels, children's excited chattering,
Eroding slowly away by the clockwork tide.

The sea is like a mirror for the twinkling stars
As the sun goes down we can already see changes.
Cross your fingers, hope and pray for the years to come,
That our haven is not taken by the millennium.

Richard Butler (12)
Ryedale School

My Life

I started off as a small little tooth,
All I heard was screaming and crying,
Moaning and groaning.
The smell of rotten old food,
Stuck in each corner and crack.

I got looser and looser, one hot summer's day
I tore into an apple
And my roots came away.
I fell on a dinner plate
And was put under a pillowcase.
That night it was dark,
Until I saw a twinkle of a wand.
I was taken away that very night.

I was pushed out by a new sparkling tooth,
He'll be starting a life like mine.
He is bigger than me
And whiter than me
And he will last for a lot longer time.
I have had my jolly old day.

Elizabeth Browning (11)
Ryedale School

WAKING UP

I open my eyes, I see the sunlight bursting
through a crack in the flowery curtains.
The smell of fresh sheets wafts past my nose,
and the scent of toast drifts upstairs.
Mum's gentle voice is muffled downstairs,
the radiator clanks and the clock is constantly
ticking.
Climbing out of bed, I feel the warm carpet on
my feet.
The icy door handle twinkles in the sunlight.
Downstairs every light is on, it's too bright.
Rushing back upstairs, I bound into bed.
The warm quilt is like a cocoon around me.
The clock's ticking slowly fades away.
I close my eyes . . .
S
l
e
e
p
i
n
g

Gemma Ford (12)
Ryedale School

AUTUMN PARK

I
wander to the nearby park on a typical autumn
evening.
Shouts and screams of the children echo in the fallen,
golden leaves.
The massive oak trees leaves are turning yellow, golden
red and brown.
The wind whistles around my ears,
Black and white border collies bark
as their owners take them for a late evening walk.
The smell of Yorkshire puds and succulent beef
simmering on the stove wafts through the walls
of the house next to the park
and fills the air.
I reach
out and
hug the
healthy
trunk of
my
favourite
oak tree.

Sally Broadbent (12)
Ryedale School

ANGER

The ancient carpet burns on the floor with its deep dark red colour.
The noise of the hoards of people shouting above each other
Resounds through my head.
All the aggravated parents and ignorant children push for the things
they want.
With the prams being knocked, comes the wails of tired and
young babies.
Which pierces your ears so they ring for minutes after.
Then there's that booming, daunting sound of the manager's voice
over the speakers
Echoes around the shop and through my head
As the customers bump each other.
They catch themselves on the edges of the shelves
And destroy their clothes with torn cotton.
When the sound has died down
And the customers return home, there is the sound of the mop
squeaking
As it is pulled along the dusty floor.

Adam Ryan (12)
Ryedale School

LONELINESS

Perched on the rocking swing.
Grasping the ice-cold chain.
The muddy field swarms with mist,
Blackbirds flock to the damp earth.
Scavenging for scraps.
The smell of ash and alcohol, poisoning my lungs.
And I am perched on the rocking swing,
Rocking, rocking, rocking.

Michael Smith (14)
Ryedale School

The Butterfly

My lord the butterfly
Has descended from his realms
To mingle with we commoners down below.
His striking cloak is
Decorated with many coal-black medals.
'He is an Admiral,' whispers my neighbour.

His shape is jagged,
But also crisp and precise.
He's highly symmetrical . . . and everyone knows it!

Now he's off again,
Drifting in the periwinkle millpond.
We sigh, watching him sail through sunbeams.

So delicate and fragile,
Yet Admiral of the garden.
He leads his fleet to destroy greenfly Armadas.

Frances Houghton (12)
Ryedale School

The Pool In The Heart Of The Woods

Broken and restless,
Cheated by life.
He stood by the side,
In the dappled moonlight.
Staring
Gazing
Dark dank depths
Waiting . . .

Emily Wilsdon (12)
Ryedale School

STAGE FRIGHT

I'm nervous
I'm really nervous,
I'm really, really nervous,
I'm just so nervous I don't think I can do this.

Here I am backstage, trembling in a corner,
My gorgeous silky costume, damp with sweat.
Outside the curtains are rising,
The crowds are yelling and applauding,
They want me!

My stomach does a somersault as I think about it,
Oh no, they are calling my name now,
Don't let this happen, I don't want to go on.

Suddenly I find myself getting up,
What has come over me?
My nervousness vanishes completely,
A feeling of excitement washes over me,
A warm glow rushes up my body.

I float on stage and burst into song,
I want this feeling to go on
                                        And on
                                                  Forever.

Sophie Collier (11)
Ryedale School

Nature

In the extremity of nature nothing is fun

In the darkest place and deepest lie
The bleeding fox too proud to cry
Hears the menacing monsters scheme
The way to make the final kill

The hawk up high with laser eye
Spots his prey from in the sky
As it scampers round in the sun
Not knowing soon its end will come

The other side of nature is very peaceful and beautiful

The cornfield shines in setting sun
The crows return as the day is done
The ripening fruit the autumn brings
Feeds birds and insects till the spring

Winter days seem long and cold
As creatures shiver in their holes
But soon the summer days will come
And warming heat will make life fun

Nature is a contrast.

Matthew Hartup (12)
Ryedale School

SHE

The hospital ward
was too cold to bare,

My sorrow took over
as I stood there.

I saw her fading
peaceful at last.

Her voice ever present
but now in the past.

The perfume I bought her
still smells so fresh,

The comfort she gave me
with every caress.

We talk much about her
each and every day,

She was my grandmother.
In my heart she will stay.

Philip Youngs (12)
Ryedale School

ALIENS

They come from a distant galaxy
Far beyond the reach of our sun
Left a planet that lay slowly dying
Where the story of life was done.

Their four eyes scoured the universe
For a place that looked fresh and new
Earth was their chosen decision
With its islands and oceans of blue.

But as they started descending
And peered out for a look around
They saw cars releasing exhaust fumes
And litter all over the ground.

And so their minds were made up
To start a search once more
They remembered a similar landscape
Do the humans know what's in store?

Jack Colman (12)
Ryedale School

WHEN I THINK OF A GARAGE, I HEAR . . .

The chatter of an engine as it tries to start,
the clanking of metal and the beep of horns.
The hum of a compressor as it buzzes like a bee,
the screeching tyres as a car spins away.

The hiss of a welder, the drip of oil and a car
growling like a dog,
growling . . . growling . . .
then it barks! Into life!

The wailing, wailing of a car alarm,
then the ping-pong sound as it is silenced.
The swish of a door as it is being shut,
then the disapproving hiss of a deflating tyre.
The click of a switch as the light goes off,
the satisfied purr of a mended car.
Like the cat that's got the cream!

Kai Smith (11)
Ryedale School

THIS FRAIL EARTH

Endless years roll on by
From the dawn of time
Until this world ends.
The sun carries on shining,
The rain will come again.
A forever changing sky
Above a sphere filled with life.
A diversity of creatures
Roaming wild and free.
From the delicate butterfly,
To the colossal blue whale.
Many different faces
Stare down the years
Contemplating the future.
One day all this will be gone,
And yet mankind hastens
To wrench this world apart.
How many more World Wars,
Nuclear explosions,
Atom bombs,
Until this frail Earth is gone?

Heather Holiday (13)
Ryedale School

All Alone!

The tiny room is cold and bare
Filled with silence
Only the distant echo of the outside
World
The floor is hard and cold.
The walls are rough
The heavy door is barred and
Bolted
A single window, darkened by years
Of dust
Outside the mountains rise into vertical
Cliffs
From the silent ground to the empty
Sky.

Becky Mason (13)
Ryedale School

Anger

A dark shed
On top of the bleak and hostile moor
Locked in
Can't escape
Piercing laughter rings through your ears
A splintery wooden floor beneath you
Sharp pains run through your feet
A stench of burnt beef lingers in the air
No way out
No way out!

Matthew Dzierzek (12)
Ryedale School

MIEGER

'I know he's in here somewhere,
I think he's over there!
Down behind the sofa,
Or underneath the chair.

He might be on the ceiling,
Or stuck beneath the floor.
I've looked under the staircase,
Now I'll look behind the door.

I'll go into my bedroom,
And look through all my drawers.
I'm sure to find him somewhere,
With his long tail and his claws.

I'll look in someone else's room,
And in the bathroom too.
I'll look right down the plughole
And even down the loo.

Mummy help me, I'm in despair
I think I've lost dear Mieger!
Stand up a minute, Mummy please . . .
You've been sitting on my tiger!'

Mary Hudson (11)
Scalby School

My Greatest Fear - The Lonely Old Woman

A silent old woman sits in a room,
A silent figure, a forgotten bloom,
Listening to silence she smiles at the stone,
Imagining the ring to her silent phone.

Sagging clothes, dust mounds of youth,
Flesh sags from bone, she licks one real tooth.
Sagged face of wrinkles, crows-feet want sleep,
From her own glazed eyes, saggy tears weep.

Half-finished pill jars sprawled on the floor,
Half-knitted jumper hung on half-opened door.
Half dreaming of half an idea of being a wife,
She spends time remember her half-lived, half-life.

Dwelling on might-have-been, unsung song,
Unwritten verse, she's dwelled for too long.
Silver hair and silver thoughts dwell in her head,
No golden lining like her mother once said.

Alone she knows little of the world and its wit,
Alone she gave love, but got none to requite,
Alone she allows the days to waste by.
The lonely old woman sits, waiting to die.

Rachel Fryirs (15)
Scalby School

THE MONSTER

On the rocky hillside I stand
My jet black hair tousled by the wind
The only place in this lonely town that will give sanctuary
to my ghastly figure.

If I dare to stand and stare,
I am shot down with hatred and disgust.
And even a child, innocent as a graceful lily,
Runs away with a fear as great as a mountain.

My only wish is to have a friend,
Someone for me to love and cherish.
Someone to live in harmony with.

But I know that the chance of this is a needle in a haystack,
Even if I travel to all four corners of the Earth,
There will never be anyone who will appreciate
the person I am,
This being the innocence of a newly opened rose . . .
I wish.

Samantha Kirby (12)
Stokesley Comprehensive School

MONSTER ON THE MOUNTAIN

Alone on the mountain,
A silent, ugly figure stands.
He is watching, waiting for a time,
When the world will accept his mind.
His stature is tall, he has long black hair,
Falling down beyond his drooping shoulders,
The unnatural figure seems
To be hoping for all his fate and neglect
To end so he can be rid of his coldness
And love the world and its people.

Now he is sitting down, he has given up.
His eyes are still open but his body has dropped.
His teeth are set in an unruly expression,
And his lips are blue, cold from rejection.
He will die unhappy, lost, to be forgotten,
Because no one will remember his
Kind heart, he was a fellow who has tried to love
But in us humans, he could not find trust.

Katie Scott (13)
Stokesley Comprehensive School

The Monster Of The Forest

The monster of the forest
All alone, all alone.
The monster of the forest
A creature of the night.
The monster of the forest
An eagle on the breeze.
The monster of the forest
The willows weep for me.
The monster of the forest
Only wanting a companion.
The monster of the forest
A killer just like man.
The monster of the forest
All alone, all alone.

Daniel Trodden (12)
Stokesley Comprehensive School

I'm Alone And Sad

A failure, that is I
I want to love
I was made to love
I should be loved.

You Frankenstein - you
You made me ugly
You made me sad.

Why, why, why?
Why should a creature be hated?
Why should a creature be sad?
Why should a creature be an outcast?

I'm alone, all alone
Alone in the world.
Alone with all my fears
Alone and sad.

They chase me
They shoot me.
Why do they hate me?

Rebecca Wake (12)
Stokesley Comprehensive School

School With Miss Draper

She was the most evil looking person that you've ever seen,
She looked what she was, horrid and mean.
She had black straight hair, scraped up in a bun.
She was tall and very thin,
Just like a sharp silver pin.
She was so silent when moving around,
You couldn't hear her at all, no not a sound.
When the bell went, into lessons we would go,
But never would we bake or sew.
She was horrid but not daft,
So all day long she'd give us maths!
I wanted my freedom, like everyone there.
I wanted to go, it wasn't fair!
All I can say to you now is
Steer clear of her - Miss Draper!

Claire Chaplain (11)
Stokesley Comprehensive School

MONSTER FEELINGS

I am different.
As I walk along a road I hear cries of terror,
Men attack me with spears, axes and sometimes guns.
If I run, they run after me.
I am too fast for them and end up hiding
in the dark covers of this desolate wood.
I need a friend,
I thought I had found some,
But they were just like the rest and made me evil
as the devil.
Violent and afraid.
I know why
Because I am hideous and people judge me unfairly.
For the first time in my short life I feel
loneliness.
Fear and sadness
I live in the wood
where no one can see me.
But I need a companion
so I will go back to my creator for a bride.

'I'm coming Frankenstein, so watch your step!'

Abi Knowles (12)
Stokesley Comprehensive School